"一带一路"
农业合作典型案例

Classic Cases of
Belt and Road
Agricultural Cooperation

农业农村部农村经济研究中心 ◎ 编

中国出版集团有限公司
研究出版社

图书在版编目（CIP）数据

"一带一路"农业合作典型案例/农业农村部农村经济研究中心编．--北京：研究出版社，2024.3
　　ISBN 978-7-5199-1650-3

　　Ⅰ.①一… Ⅱ.①农… Ⅲ.①"一带一路"—农业合作—国际合作—案例 Ⅳ.① F31
　　中国国家版本馆 CIP 数据核字 (2024) 第 054489 号

出 品 人：陈建军
出版统筹：丁　波
责任编辑：寇颖丹　范存刚
助理编辑：何雨格

一带一路
YIDAI YILU
农业合作典型案例

研究出版社　出版发行
（100006　北京市东城区灯市口大街 100 号华腾商务楼）
北京新华印刷有限公司印刷　新华书店经销
2024 年 3 月第 1 版　2024 年 3 月第 1 次印刷
开本：710 毫米 ×1000 毫米　1/16　印张：12.5
字数：174 千字
ISBN 978-7-5199-1650-3　定价：58.00 元
电话（010）64217619　64217652（发行部）

版权所有·侵权必究
凡购买本社图书，如有印制质量问题，我社负责调换。

《"一带一路"农业合作典型案例》
编委人员

金文成　陈　洁　翟雪玲　原瑞玲
炎天尧　聂赟彬　陈　龙

目录

1 南南合作助力乌干达减贫与发展
　　——中国—联合国粮农组织—乌干达南南合作项目 ……………… 001

2 携手打造国际分工合作平台
　　——中印尼"两国双园"合作项目 …………………………………… 009

3 践行"一带一路"倡议,共创"甜"蜜事业
　　——埃塞俄比亚糖厂项目 ……………………………………………… 017

4 推动"文莱—广西经济走廊"建设
　　——海世通文莱渔业项目 ……………………………………………… 025

5 借鉴中国经验,助推老挝乡村振兴
　　——"亚钾国际"促进老挝乡村发展 ………………………………… 033

6 金融活水助力企业乘风破浪"走出去"
　　——金融机构支持企业开展国际合作 ………………………………… 041

7 探索"粮食安全"供应链新模式
　　——爱菊中哈粮油合作项目 ···································· 049

8 共建防灾减灾体系，携手保护生态环境
　　——中哈农业旱灾与虫灾监测预警项目 ······················ 057

9 技术引领，构建人类命运共同体
　　——菌草技术援外实践 ·· 065

10 凝心聚力，打造中国援外技术品牌
　　——布隆迪高级农业专家技术援助项目 ······················ 073

Contents

1 South–South Cooperation Contributes to Uganda's Poverty Reduction and Development

—China-FAO-Uganda South-South Cooperation ················ 083

2 Working Together for A Platform of Global Division of Labor and Cooperation

—China-Indonesia "Two Countries, Twin Parks" Project ················ 093

3 "Sweet" Cooperation under the Belt and Road Initiative

—Ethiopian Sugar Factory Project ················ 105

4 Advancement of Brunei–Guangxi Economic Corridor (BGEC)

—Hiseaton Fisheries (B) Sdn Bhd Project ················ 115

5 Boosting Rural Revitalization of Laos with China's Experience

— "Asia-Potash" Working for Rural Development of Laos ················ 125

6 Financial Resources Empower Enterprises to Go Global

—Financial Institutions Support Enterprises in Their International Cooperation ················ 137

7 Exploring a New Model of "Food Security" Supply Chain

—Aiju Sino-Kazakhstan Grain and Oil Cooperation Project ····················· 149

8 Building the China–Kazakhstan System for Preventing and Mitigating Natural Disasters

—A Bilateral Project for Monitoring and Early Warning Agricultural Drought and Pests ·· 159

9 Technologically Build a Human Community with a Shared Future

—Foreign Aid through JUNCAO Technology ······································ 169

10 Gathering Strengths to Build Chinese Brand for Foreign Technology Assistance

—Technology assistance to Burundi by senior Chinese agricultural experts ··· 181

南南合作助力乌干达减贫与发展

——中国—联合国粮农组织—乌干达南南合作项目

南南合作助力乌干达减贫与发展
——中国—联合国粮农组织—乌干达南南合作项目

乌干达具有得天独厚的自然气候条件，农牧业在乌干达国民经济中占主导地位，但其农业基础条件差，生产以小农户为主，农业发展受到财政、技术、投资、耕作方式等多方面限制，部分地区人口仍然面临粮食短缺的问题。乌干达是首批中国—联合国粮农组织南南合作计划支持的国家之一，在2012—2018年，乌干达执行了两期南南合作项目。该项目将中国农业技术和发展经验与乌干达实际相结合，传授新技术、推广新品种和分享新理念，联合国粮农组织副总干事贝丝·贝克多表示，该项目是中国—联合国粮农组织南南合作计划下持续时间最长、最成功的国家项目。

一、基本情况

在中国—联合国粮农组织南南合作框架下，中国政府分别于2012—2014年、2016—2018年在乌干达开展了两期南南合作项目，在谷物、园艺、水产、畜牧等方面提供技术支持，提高生产能力，保障食品安全，同时通过发展农业价值链，提高农产品附加值，吸引农业投资，促进农民增收。在一期项目取得积极成效的基础上，二期项目主要支持《乌农业领域发展规划（2016—2020）》，重点领域包括园艺、谷物、水产、畜牧、农业综合经营。两期项目中，中国政府共计派出47名农业专家和技术员向乌干达提供技术支持，将中国农业技术和发展经验与乌干达实际相结合，传授新技术、推广新品种和分享新理念，帮助乌干达提升粮食安全水平和农业综合生产能力。项目取得良好政治、经济、社会效益，乌总统专门致信中国国家主席习近平盛赞项目成果并希望启动新一期项目，得到了习近平主席积极回应。乌干达项目是首个合作国与东道国元首皆予以书面赞誉的南南合作项目，也是首个利用信托基金开展第三期合作的项目。在联合国粮农组织积极协调下，乌干达政府决定出资约962万美元，在联合国粮农组织设立单边信托基金用于支持即将开展的中国—联合国粮农组织—乌干达（第三期）南南合作项目。这是迄今为止，中国—联合国粮农组织南南合作框架下，东道国政府提供的最大规模捐款，也是成功利用中国—联合国粮农组织南南合作信托基金撬动东道国资金支持，发挥东道国主观能动性的典范。

二、主要做法

南南合作在乌干达的成功实践，得益于双方认真落实有关发展理念，将中国农业技术和发展经验与乌干达实际相结合，明确主体责任、创新发展模式、注重能力建设。

一是明确各合作主体的责任和义务，共同制定项目规划。联合国粮农组织总部和驻华代表处分别成立联合国粮农组织南南合作项目管理团队，负责总部、区域和次区域的相关部门联络。中国农业农村部和中国常驻联合国粮农机构代表处组成中方南南合作项目管理团队，负责项目的具体实施、协调和跟进，以及建立统一的标准和实施方法。乌干达农牧渔业部负责南南合作项目的执行。中、乌、联合国粮农组织三方共同协调制定项目规划，包括预规划和"三方联合规划设计"两部分。通过规划设计，明确各方责任，收集乌干达农牧渔业发展和粮食安全重点领域正在执行的项目信息，查明可以作为项目参与单位的机构和工作点，为必要的实地考察和技术会议做好前期准备。

二是中方专家组提供技术支持，探索新型农业模式。完成项目规划等前期准备后，中国派出专家组赴乌干达开展技术援助，通过实施示范项目、推广实用农业技术、引进优良品种，开展调查研究，在水果、蔬菜、食用菌、稻田养鱼等领域提高乌干达农业生产水平；农业技术则涉及杂交水稻、狐尾小米、病虫害管理等。在做好生产指导的同时，中国专家组通过红薯粉、牛肉干等农牧加工示范项目延长价值链；通过"企业+农户"方式拓宽市场销售渠道；通过指导"稻田养鱼""中国模式沼气""循环农业""休闲农业"等方式，开启了当地农业新模式，全面提高农业的经济、社会与生态效益。

三是中方提供渠道以加强乌方能力建设。能力建设主要包括实地培训和访华考察团两种形式。实地培训的模式多种多样，因地制宜。内容包括园艺、畜牧、杂交水稻、狐尾小米、水产养殖、沼气技术等。项目访华考察内容主要涉及中国农业发展、项目实施管理、科技示范推广、农牧业生产模式、品种资源、价值链开发、企业投资等。

三、成效及展望

中乌南南合作项目通过技术推广、建设中乌农业合作产业园的方式，全面提升乌干达农牧渔业的技术水平，并提高贫困人口的生产生活质量。

一是多领域技术生产水平明显提升。该项目为乌干达在多领域提供了技术、能力等方面的支持，有效提升了其在农牧渔业领域的生产能力和粮食安全水平，经济效益明显，推动了乌农民增收和农村减贫。第一，有效提升粮食生产能力。通过南南合作技术援助，乌杂交水稻产量达9~10吨/公顷，约为本地高产品种的3倍；杂交小米产量为当地常规品种的2~3倍；项目的示范作用带动了乌境内10多个行政区生产小米 70 公顷，杂交水稻 60 公顷，促进了当地农民增收、粮食自给自足，提高了农业生产能力，极大地增强了乌发展农业、提高粮食安全水平的信心。第二，园艺新型技术在大面积生产应用中极有价值。专家组指导乌农科院繁育苹果砧木 150 万株，是过去四年总量的 2 倍；开展食用菌、马铃薯试验生产及杧果实蝇、柑橘黑斑病的防治试验，在大面积生产应用中极有价值。第三，扩大了畜牧养殖规模。专家组设计利用氨化饲料、种植象草以解决饲料质量和旱季缺草问题，提高秸秆的营养价值，增加牲畜的可食性和适口性；针对进口鸡笼成本高、养殖户难以承担的问题，专家组自行设计木制鸡笼并积极推广，对扩大养殖规模和集约化生产提供了有效手段。第四，开发了新型水产养殖方式。渔场设计、鱼苗孵化、幼苗运输、鱼塘设计及养殖、稻田养鱼、饲料加工等 6 个示范项目，使小规模饲料加工产量每天达到 800 千克，使鱼苗孵化率从 20% 提高到 80%、幼苗运输成活率从 79% 提高到 98% 以上。稻田养鱼已成为当地农民增收致富的一种新型生产方式。

中国专家组示范的杂交水稻获丰收

二是中乌农业合作产业园建设全面提高生产生活质量。该项目将发展合作和投资促进相结合，在为乌农业发展提供实用农业技术的同时，通过引入私营部门、建设中乌农业合作产业园等方式，有效地改善了当地的基础设施，延长了农业生产价值链，全面提高了农民的生产生活质量。第一，解决了当地农业生产的技术、农资与市场问题。园区采用"公司＋农户"模式，为当地农民提供良种、农资及免费技术服务，同时按照合同收购农产品，搭建农户与市场之间的桥梁。目前已为当地840公顷水稻种植区提供必要的物资供应与技术指导，形成了以核心园区为龙头，梯次辐射带动当地农业发展的局面。第二，改善了农业农村基础设施，保障了农业生产和民生。园区投资20万美元在附近打机井3口、建水池4个，解决了周边1200多户村民的生产生活用水问题，受到了当地民众的热烈欢迎。第三，增加了就业机会，拓宽了农民增收渠道。目前，园区在当地招聘留学欧美本科以上学历的中层管理者6人；聘用专门从事示范区工程与田间管理工作的当地长期雇员216人；由于农业生产的季节性，临时聘用人员达1000人次以上。当地人都以进入园区工作为荣。随着园区建设的不断推进，计划将带动当地直接就业人数逾万人。

2009年以来，中国、乌干达、联合国粮农组织一直在进行南南合作，以解决影响农作物、渔业和畜牧业等关键农业领域及农产品的首要制约因素。项目的前两期取得了令人瞩目的成果，为了全面提高乌干达农业生产水平，三方于2023年启动了第三期项目，将主要聚焦四大领域，建立一个综合技术转让基地，制订水稻和小米高产计划，支持畜牧业改良计划，发展水产养殖价值链，旨在巩固扩大前两期的成效，更大范围推广中国先进适用技术，帮助乌干达从解决温饱的农业向商业化的农业转变。

携手打造国际分工合作平台

——中印尼"两国双园"合作项目

携手打造国际分工合作平台
——中印尼"两国双园"合作项目

福建是 21 世纪海上丝绸之路核心区,与东盟经贸合作与交流密切。印尼是福建籍华侨华人主要聚集地,双方之间的交流源远流长。2018 年著名侨乡福清市提出中国—印度尼西亚"两国双园"(以下简称中印尼"两国双园")设想,探索建立产业互联、设施互通、政策互惠的双园结对合作机制。中方以元洪投资区为主体,印尼方以民丹工业园、阿维尔那工业园和巴塘工业园为主体,构建以产业链、供应链为主的国际分工合作平台,打造中—印尼之间投资贸易绿色通道,使"两国双园"成为承接"一带一路"倡议下相关合作项目的重要平台。

一、基本情况

"两国双园"是指两个主权国家在对方境内互设园区、联动发展的一种新型产能合作方式。结合两国发展战略和双边经贸合作情况,中印尼"两国双园"合作项目旨在将园区建设成为立足新发展阶段、贯彻新发展理念、构建新发展格局、深化面向东盟的跨境合作的经贸创新发展示范园区;推动打造稳固高效的特色产业链、供应链、价值链的国际分工合作创新模式,构建国内国际双循环重要战略通道,更好地落实新一轮对外开放合作的先行示范园区;建设"专业、创新、绿色、开放"的国际化高端园区,构建大宗食品、食材、水果、肉类等集散关键枢纽和双循环重要通道。通过合作全面深化中国与印尼的经贸、人文往来，立足福建华侨华人遍布全球各地的优势，塑造侨乡品牌、弘扬侨乡文化、展示侨乡亲情，推动经贸创新发展示范区成为新老侨胞回归创业的热土，打造华侨华人密切交流交往的新窗口，打造中印尼服务贸易和投资合作的新平台，打造中印尼经济合作和高端产业合作的新高地。

目前，中印尼"两国双园"中方园区围绕海洋经济、食品加工、跨境贸易等重点领域，延伸拓展产业链，加快推进海洋渔业、装备制造、清真食品、冷链物流、绿色矿业、轻纺等产业合作，与印尼方面共同打造"全球渔业中心"和海洋经济发展新高地。

二、主要做法

中印尼"两国双园"探索建立产业互联、设施互通、政策互惠的双园结对合作机制，采用中国与印尼在对方境内互设园区、联动发展的新型产能合作模式，对于促成两国优势互补、盘活两国优势资源、完善两国相关产业链供应链、促进两国经贸往来具有重要意义。

一是完善工作机制。中印尼"两国双园"建立了中印尼"两国双园"联合工作委员会和副部（省）级磋商机制，并形成商务部、福建省、福州市、福清市多级联动机制，统筹推动园区建设。省级层面，福建省成立了推进"两国双园"建设工作领导小组，由常务副省长、分管副省长担任组长，组建了工作专班，实行周会商制度。市级层面，福州市成立了工作领导小组和经贸对接小组，全方位整合资源力量，高效协调推动各项工作落实。福清市创新"指挥部+管委会+投资公司+产业基金+智库"开发运作模式，成立"两国双园"控股集团，全面推进园区高水平标准化建设。

二是建立对话机制。2021年以来，商务部会同福建省人民政府推动与印尼有关部门建立畅通的对话机制。2021年3月23日，商务部原副部长张向晨会同福建省副省长郭宁宁与印尼海洋与投资统筹部副部长欧迪·卡拉克以视频形式共同主持召开中印尼"两国双园"联合工作委员会第一次会议，双方共同宣布正式启动"两国双园"联合工作委员会机制。2023年6月16日，商务部亚洲司及中国驻印尼大使馆经商处，福建省商务厅、外办及福州市和福州海关，印尼海统部三方召开了推进中印尼"两国双园"建设工作层磋商会，达成了5项共识。2023年8月31日，中印尼"两国双园"联合工作委员会第二次会议在福州市召开，福州市政府、印尼方园区代表分别提出了需相互协同推动的工作事项，围绕园区管理机构联合工作机制、编制园区发展规划、推进贸易投资便利化、支持政策等方面进行了深入细致的交流沟通，对双方园区建设下一步合作内容达成了共识。

三是强化政策赋能。为进一步推动资源向园区集聚，将中方园区打造成高质量发展的政策"洼地"、开放"高地"、投资"宝地"、发展"福地"，福建省商务厅牵头研提了一批省级专项政策举措，同时向国家部委争取了部分政策措施，主要涉及要素保障、产业政策、财税政策、通关政策、人才政策等方面，目前正在按流程申报和审定印发实施。另外，福建省还将于近期颁布实施《中国—印度尼西亚经贸创新发展示范园区建设实施方案》《中国—印度尼西亚经贸创新发展示范园区建设省级专项政策措施》。

三、成效及展望

一是拉动中国与印尼投资规模持续扩大。自中印尼"两国双园"获批以来，一批重大项目集中开工、投产，有力提升了双方的产业承载能力。2023年以来，中印尼"两国双园"建设驶入"快车道"。2023年2月，印尼—福州经贸对接会暨项目签约活动在印尼雅加达举行，集中签约15宗项目，总投资216亿元；5月，中国（福建）—印尼共建"两国双园"暨经贸合作推介会在印尼雅加达举行，21个项目现场签约，签约总金额达432亿元；8月6日在福州举行的中国（福建）—东盟经贸合作论坛上，又有9个项目集中签约，涉及总投资近300亿元。截至2023年8月，中方园区已进驻商贸企业620家，投资项目66个，总投资905.51亿元；中方园区企业赴印尼投资项目17宗，总投资399.3亿元。

中方园区—福州元洪投资区鸟瞰图

二是助推双边经贸关系迈上新台阶。受"两国双园"合作项目带动，中国（主要是福建省）与印尼经贸合作快速发展，2022年印尼已成为福建在东盟的第一大贸易伙伴，进出口贸易达1215.2亿元，同比增长32.2%。中国连续8年保持印尼最大贸易伙伴地位，持续保持印尼第三大外资来源国地位。印尼《雅加达邮报》刊文称，过去20年来，中国一直是印尼最重要的合作伙伴，特别是在经济发展、投资和贸易等领域。在中国"一带一路"倡议和印尼"全球海洋支点"构想的支持下，中印尼两国将在基础设施领域加强合作。

三是促进双方交流合作日益紧密。"两国双园"合作项目推动双方海上互联互通，促进投资和贸易，增进人文交流与合作。双方合作主要聚焦海洋渔业、矿业、基础设施、文化旅游等领域，并开拓了双方在清洁能源、新型材料、纺织等领域的合作潜力。目前，福建省已成立多个印尼研究中心，高校已开设印尼语专业，印尼来华留学生数量日渐增长，教育合作为双方增进了解、促进友好往来播下了种子。

从后期发展态势看，未来中印尼"两国双园"将继续以和平合作、开放包容、互学互鉴、互利共赢的丝绸之路精神为指引，全方位加强"两国双园"共商、共建，共享"两国双园"发展成果，实现双方园区"互利共赢"。

一是在政策方面争取更大突破。在投资贸易准入、注册申报流程、人才跨境互认、远洋捕捞、水产养殖、通关便利、税收优惠等方面，出台支持印尼方园区建设的政策措施，吸引更多中方企业落户印尼方园区。

二是着力扶引龙头，壮大产业集群。以海洋渔业为突破口，围绕中印尼海洋渔业、热带农业、轻工纺织、机械电子、绿色矿业五大产业，培育中印尼两国合作产业链供应链。扶大扶强龙头企业，加强以商招商，推动延链补链强链，以龙头企业落地带动上下游企业入驻，推动扩大双向贸易规模，实现园区产业集群发展。

三是推进目标事项取得新成效。推动成立中印尼"两国双园"产业合作促进中心，成立中印尼"两国双园"海关联合工作小组，建立中印尼海关协调机制等，促进双方海关加强沟通、协同互助。

3

践行"一带一路"倡议,共创"甜"蜜事业

——埃塞俄比亚糖厂项目

践行"一带一路"倡议，共创"甜"蜜事业
——埃塞俄比亚糖厂项目

中国和埃塞俄比亚都是文明古国，两国交往历史悠久，源远流长，双方关系一直是中非合作的典范。尤其在"一带一路"倡议下，中埃的合作领域更加广泛。2013年以来，中国机械工业集团有限公司下属企业中工国际工程股份有限公司（以下简称中工国际）积极践行"一带一路"倡议，深入埃塞俄比亚，开展食糖产业合作，取得了非常好的社会效益，树立了中非合作的典范，展现了我国良好的国际形象。

一、基本情况

埃塞俄比亚的咖啡闻名世界，埃塞俄比亚人也酷爱咖啡，糖是埃塞俄比亚人日常生活必需品。但由于生产能力不足，埃塞俄比亚食糖供给缺口非常大。埃塞俄比亚人口超1亿人，按照非洲区域平均消费量每人每年14千克食糖计算，埃塞俄比亚每年对食糖的需求量约140万吨，但本国食糖年产量只有不到30万吨，缺口超110万吨。尽管当地气候土壤条件适合甘蔗种植，但由于食糖加工产能低和技术缺乏，埃塞俄比亚每年需花费宝贵的数亿美元外汇进口白糖。因此，增加制糖产能、提高制糖技术是埃塞俄比亚迫在眉睫的战略需求。2009年，埃塞俄比亚国内陆续开始糖厂建设，还从农民手里征收了大量土地用于种植甘蔗。但由于项目建设和管理问题，误期和超支严重，糖厂建

设被迫停工。

中工国际践行"一带一路"倡议，聚焦设计咨询与工程承包、先进工程技术装备开发与应用、工程投资与运营三大业务板块，为客户提供勘察设计、规划咨询、融资投资、成套设备采购供应、施工与项目管理、运营维护等综合服务。中工国际在了解到埃塞俄比亚食糖产业的发展规划后，主动作为，周密计划，决定帮助埃塞俄比亚发展壮大食糖产业。中工国际发挥专业优势，于2013年首次承建埃塞俄比亚北部的24000TCD的瓦尔凯特糖厂，因高效的建设进度和过硬的公司实力获得了埃塞俄比亚政府和社会的高度肯定和赞扬。在此背景下，受埃塞俄比亚糖业集团的委托，中工国际于2019年接手埃塞俄比亚糖业集团未完成的贝雷斯1号糖厂建设任务。经过2年紧锣密鼓地建设，中工国际克服了新冠疫情大流行、埃塞俄比亚内战影响和材料短缺等重重困难，完成了项目建设。2021年6月6日，贝雷斯1号糖厂正式投入运营并正式出糖。2022年5月，中工国际受业主埃塞俄比亚糖业集团邀请，成功签署了该项目的运营合同。2023年4月，在完成了项目的完工测试和性能测试后，中工国际再次受业主委托，签署了该项目的2023年运营合同。

二、主要做法

项目自建设以来，中工国际从项目管理团队成立、商务合同管理、分包商招标、项目执行实施、人才培养、项目成本控制、质量及安全管理和品牌树立等方面全方位、多角度参与项目建设。

一是统筹谋划布局，打造全流程管理模式。在项目开发设计初期，中工国际对项目设计情况、设备条件、施工状况等情况进行了现场考察，收集资料和深度分析，快速又专业地完成了项目补充设计和设备选型，确定合理的施工方案。该项目采用印度的概念设计，设备来自德国、中国、印度等多个国家。在执行中，各专业组深入消化原技术思路，了解设备特点，结合现场实际和未来运营需要，组织相关人员开展精细化施工，成功完成了各系统续建工作。积极加强与当地政府和业主的深度高效沟通，实现作业规范、技术管控有力，得到了监理和业主的高度评价。项目部技术人员因地制宜，结合国内糖厂生产运营经验，对原有工艺和老旧设备提出改进意见，累计提出1000余个改进建议和措施，提高了工作效率。

埃塞俄比亚贝雷斯1号糖厂鸟瞰图

二是深植可持续发展战略，重视绿色施工。中工国际坚持环保领跑、效益领先的科学建设之路，以可持续发展的思路引导项目建设。在项目实施中融合了公司"绿色设计、绿色工程、绿色制造和绿色产业"的"四绿"理念，打造绿色环保精品工程。项目包含一座日处理可达6000立方米的污水处理站，中工国际项目部定时检测排水的BOD、COD5和溶解氧等指标，确保排放废水达到灌溉用水标准。处理后的废水可直接浇灌甘蔗地，保护了当地生态环境的同时也节约了水资源。此外,中工国际还制定了多项施工环保管理措施,如废土弃运、建筑垃圾和安装耗材废料外运、场区扬尘治理、废气废水排放等,配备专职安全管理团队专项监督,形成常态机制,确保各类环保措施落实到位。

三是推进共建共享共赢,支持属地化协同发展。埃塞俄比亚工业发展相对落后,糖厂领域的专业设备大多依赖进口。中工国际项目部坚持共建共享共赢的原则,因地制宜,将中国先进的施工技术和工艺方法与埃塞俄比亚工程实际相结合,既满足了规范要求,也保证了工期,为项目的顺利推进提供了优质的工程服务。项目在土建、电气安装、结构安装、保温工程等方面大量选用本地施工企业,带动了本土企业的发展。其中,"ABIYU ILLU CONTRACTOR"便是优秀属地分包商的代表。此外,中工国际在管理人员和施工队伍招收上,也尽量实现属地化管理、属地化运行。建设高峰期时,现场1000多工人里有800多都是当地工人,积极为当地民众提供就业岗位。

埃塞俄比亚青少年手捧白糖

三、成效及展望

一是缩小埃塞俄比亚食糖缺口，节省大量外汇。贝雷斯1号糖厂满负荷运转状态下，可实现日榨甘蔗1.2万吨，日产精糖1500吨，年产白糖20万吨，每年节省外汇1.2亿美元。这些节省的外汇被用以进口食用油、小麦等其他急缺的粮食作物和产品，为整个国家的持续发展创造了有利条件。

二是拓宽就业渠道，助力人才培养。贝雷斯1号糖厂项目为当地提供了大量就业机会。在运营期，贝雷斯1号糖厂可解决5000个甘蔗种植工，4000名甘蔗收割工，1000名糖厂运营技术工人的就业。建设期和运营期带动了建筑材料和施工耗材等上下游企业的发展，也促进了当地社区经济、住房、餐饮、畜牧、社区医疗和教育等行业的快速发展。同时，项目运营期，20余名工程师和70余名运营工人的中方团队通过两班倒的不间断值班，将先进的制糖工艺和热电站操作技术传授给了当地工程师和工人，为埃塞俄比亚培养了大批制糖专业技术人员，还为当地培养了大批熟练施工技术人才，提高当地管理水平和技术水平。

三是实现绿色低碳与经济效益有机结合。贝雷斯1号糖厂利用锅炉焚烧甘蔗渣发电和产生蒸汽，电和汽满足工艺设备生产需要，产生的二氧化碳等又被种植的甘蔗吸收，工艺副产品废蜜可制作饲料和酒精，滤泥和灰渣经处理又可作为甘蔗生长的肥料，是名副其实的绿色工厂。糖厂的两个25MW发电机组在保证糖厂生产用电的同时，可以每天对外发电240MWH，缓解了当地电网的用电压力，每年可产生经济效益约60万美元。

四是创造和传递中国精品工程价值。贝雷斯1号糖厂项目积极服务国家外交大局和响应"一带一路"倡议，受到埃塞俄比亚国家电视台、《人民日报》、新华网、中央广播电视总台等国内外主流媒体的广泛关注和多次报道，也得到了埃塞俄比亚各界的一致好评。埃塞俄比亚总理阿比·艾哈迈德曾表示该项目承载了埃塞俄比亚人民的希望，是"实实在在的民生工程"，州市等各级政府将糖厂作为不同学龄学子的教育基地。

埃塞俄比亚贝雷斯1号糖厂项目实现性能测试和生产运营是埃塞俄比亚糖业发展史上浓墨重彩的一笔，也是中工国际深耕非洲市场投建营一体化的重要转折点。

未来，中工国际将秉承共商、共建、共享原则，继续深化与埃塞俄比亚和非洲其他国家在制糖领域的战略合作，全面推动当地的经济社会发展，积极履行社会责任，大力支持全球减贫事业，努力把每一个项目建设成为沟通两国民心的纽带和深化友谊的桥梁，高水平参与共建"一带一路"，为人类命运共同体贡献力量和智慧。

推动"文莱—广西经济走廊"建设

——海世通文莱渔业项目

推动"文莱—广西经济走廊"建设
——海世通文莱渔业项目

文莱是东盟国家中与中国外交关系良好、交流合作频繁的国家。"一带一路"倡议提出以来，中文两国经贸合作快速拓展，"文莱—广西经济走廊"作为中国文莱合作的两大旗舰项目之一稳步推进。广西海世通食品股份有限公司承担实施的文莱—中国（广西）渔业合作示范区项目是"文莱—广西经济走廊"框架下的首个落地项目，在国家和广西壮族自治区的大力推动下，项目顺利实施并取得卓著成效。

一、基本情况

广西海世通食品股份有限公司主要从事海水水产品养殖、加工、国内外销售业务，2009年开始建设离岸大型网箱，进行海水鱼类研发和养殖，是广西第一家规模化从事大型网箱海水养殖的企业。近年来，公司为了规避自然台风灾害，寻求更好的发展空间，同时积极响应国家"一带一路"倡议，实施"走出去"发展计划，在海外寻找适宜发展海洋养殖产业的地方。自2012年起，经过在东盟多个国家的反复考察，最终确认文莱是最佳的深海网箱养殖地。文莱属热带雨林气候，海水温度常年恒定在28℃，且水文条件良好，水域无污染、无台风，非常适宜开展网箱养殖。但文莱当地的养殖技术落后，渔业技术人员缺乏，外海养殖存在诸多亟待解决的技术问题，当地存在强烈的招商引资、带动产业发展的现实诉求。

在国家有政策、文莱有需求、企业有诉求的背景下，广西壮族自治区政府、文莱政府和广西海世通公司积极推动双边合作，通过多次交流洽谈，广西海世通公司和文莱方面达成共识，于2016年6月与文莱政府部门签署了合作框架性协议。在合作框架下，由广西海世通公司出资1000万元在文莱投资成立海世通渔业（文莱）有限公司[Hiseaton Fisheries（B）SdnBhd]，从事海洋水产品的种苗繁育、养殖、收购、加工与销售业务。文莱政府批复给予海世通渔业（文莱）有限公司2000公顷外海海域使用权和22公顷育苗场加工用地及2公顷产品加工用地，同时将文莱国家渔业发展中心以较低租金提供给海世通文莱公司使用。

文莱—中国（广西）渔业合作示范区项目总投资1.3亿元，由一个中心和四个功能区构成，即水产科技联合研究中心、深海网箱养殖基地、饲料和产品加工基地、苗种繁育基地、仓储物流基地，总面积达20.2平方公里，分两个五年计划实施。截至目前，公司已经完成一期工程建设，建成种苗繁育基地和海上网箱养殖基地，保障了养殖品种的保种选育工作。

二、主要做法

文莱虽有丰富的渔业资源，但渔业基础薄弱，产业配套设施不健全，产业链供应链不完善，缺乏养殖技术。海世通文莱公司在文莱政府授权下开展相关基础设施的投资建设，并招募团队进行研发繁育工作，同时依托国内广西海世通公司多年的养殖技术积累和与中国水产科学院的合作机制，为文莱—中国（广西）渔业合作示范区项目提供技术支撑，实现养殖技术的本土化，并广泛开展技术培训。海世通文莱公司在将中国的先进技术带到文莱，带动文莱渔业发展的同时，也把文莱的研究成果经验贡献给中国渔业，真正实现了互通发展经验，共享发展成果。

一是开展基础设施建设，为产业发展提供基础支撑。文莱渔业产业基础薄弱，缺乏开展本地苗种繁育的基础设施。要在文莱进行渔业养殖首先需要建设相关繁育养殖基地。海世通文莱渔业项目主要由苗种繁育中心、深水网箱养殖平台和一个国际研发交流培训中心构成，其中苗种繁育中心和深水网箱养殖平台构成产业核心区，国际研发交流培训中心构成研发示范区。产业核心区主要包含亲本培育区、苗种饵料生物培养区、苗种培育区、大规模苗种培育区、商品鱼养殖区、产品加工区六个部分，亲本培育区提供催产孵化的鱼苗受精卵，饵料区进行饲料配套，苗种培育区、大规模苗种培育区分别对孵化后的仔稚鱼、大规模鱼苗进行培育，商品鱼养殖区进行商品鱼的养成，产品加工区完成从深水网箱平台处的"捕捞—运输—前处理—急冻—冷藏—检测—出库"流程。在上述基础设施建设的支持下，海世通文莱公司在文莱水产功能区组成了一个"原种—种苗—养殖—饲料—加工"完整的产业链。

大规格商品鱼深海养殖基地

二是依托国内企业技术积累，实现技术的本土化转化。要在文莱扎根，除了完成上述基础设施建设外，技术起到举足轻重的作用。从初期保证鱼苗进口的存活率，到后续养殖、繁育，都离不开技术的支持。但文莱本土缺乏相应技术，又因文莱的气候、水文条件与中国不同，所以无法将中国的技术全盘应用于文莱。为解决这一难题，海世通文莱公司借助中国母公司的资源，多年来与中国水产科学院等专业机构建立长期的紧密合作关系，多次邀请专家到文莱因地制宜地进行指导与培训，通过不断的技术调整，首次实现了鱼苗供给本地化，为当地渔业可持续发展提供了有力支撑。

三是充分开展合作交流，培养当地渔业人才。渔业产业的长期发展离不开渔业人才。海世通文莱公司作为牵头单位，联合文莱科研机构如文莱大学、文莱国家渔业发展中心、IBTE等，中国国内高校科研院所如上海海洋大学、中国水产科学研究院等，共同发起中文渔业科技合作平台。目前，海世通文莱公司与文莱技术大学、文莱大学和文莱职业技术学院达成合作意向，在公司的科研中心和养殖基地设立教学、实习基地，公司技术人员被聘任为兼职教师，为文莱水产人才的培养和教育提供公益服务。此外，示范区与国内的广西水产科学研究院、中国水产科学院南海水产研究所等科研机构开展了稳定深入合作，引入国内优秀人才入园进行共同研究，将国内的优良技术在示范区内进行转化落地，不断提升平台的研发实力，扩大平台在东南亚的影响力。自2016年以来，为解决当地渔业技术人员短缺问题，海世通文莱公司开始针对本地及东增区赴文务工渔民开展职业技术培训。多年来，该培训逐渐形成了较好的品牌效应。海世通文莱公司并与文莱水产养殖发展中心、三亚热带水产研究院、文莱大学等科研机构达成共识，将进一步提升培训层次和范围。

三、成效及展望

在中文两国政府和相关部门的支持下，目前示范区建设进展良好，在文莱养殖领域也创造了辉煌的成绩。本项目的实施在带动文莱渔业产业发展、促进我国外交事业发展和推动"一带一路"倡议落地等方面作出了积极贡献。在带动当地渔业发展方面，海世通文莱公司的入驻在文莱实现了三个"第一"：

一是第一次实现了**本地化苗种供应**。结束了文莱本国鱼类养殖苗种需要进口的历史，并成功开展了经济热带鱼类的综合人工养殖。二是**建立了第一个外海海洋牧场**。在文莱外海有关海域建设安装并投入使用了大型网箱24口、小型网箱178口，打破了文莱外海海洋牧场零建设的历史。三是**第一次将海水养殖鱼类出口到加拿大、美国等国家**。

渔业作为我国重要的出口主导型产业，在农业对外合作中起先锋作用。广西海世通公司近年来发展迅速，对外合作程度加深，作为"走出去"企业的典范，在带动当地产业发展的同时，注重从事本地人才培养等公益性活动，践行合作双赢理念，为加强同"一带一路"沿线国家合作交流提供了成功案例，增强了主权国家间各经营主体开展合作、互利共赢的信心。

未来，示范区将以深海网箱养殖为先导，以品种选育、繁育为基础，以科研攻关为保障，以产业化开发为主线，建立起品种选育、种苗繁育、养殖、饲料生产、加工销售"一体化"产业链模式，带动制造、渔需服务、贸易和运输等相关产业的发展。一是完善配套设施，完成加工厂、制冰厂设施设备的安装及运作，提升企业硬件运作能力。二是建立示范区管理机构和管理机制，提高管理团队的国际化和专业化水平。三是建立专家咨询制度和人才引进培养制度，提升示范区科技创新能力。四是建立政策咨询、投资分析、资金筹措、生产服务、风险防范、产品营销、技术标准、质量安全、信息联络等服务体系，促进产业聚集，提升产业国际竞争力。

5

借鉴中国经验，助推老挝乡村振兴

——"亚钾国际"促进老挝乡村发展

借鉴中国经验，助推老挝乡村振兴
——"亚钾国际"促进老挝乡村发展

亚钾国际投资股份有限公司（以下简称亚钾国际）是一家专业从事钾盐开采、钾肥生产及销售的国际化企业。公司专注老挝钾盐行业14年，是老挝的标杆中资企业。亚钾国际在老挝生产钾肥的同时，高度关注老挝农业和乡村发展，通过深入挖掘老挝农业资源潜力，发展现代农业，开展产业扶贫，投身当地公益事业，对促进老挝乡村发展，树立充满活力、和合共生、负责任有担当的中国企业形象，夯实两国合作基础发挥了积极作用。

一、基本情况

亚钾国际是老挝第一家实现工业化开采的钾盐企业。2020年，公司启动100万吨钾盐项目，仅历时17个月就完成了建设、调试、达产达标，创造了"亚钾速度"。2022年12月31日，第二个100万吨钾肥项目也投建完成，成为东南亚规模最大的钾肥企业。目前，第三个百万吨钾盐建设项目已经启动，预计2023年底将实现300万吨产能，2025年实现500万吨钾肥产能，届时将成为世界级钾肥供应商。亚钾国际的钾肥除了供应东南亚各国，也一直供应国内，是国内钾肥进口的重要来源。

老挝是东南亚唯一的内陆国，农业完全靠天吃饭，水利灌溉设施薄弱，病虫害频发，技术水平落后。目前，老挝农业仍然停留在广种薄收的小农经济生产方式上，效益低下，农民收入水平低，生活水平低，农村地区的贫困发生率在30%左右。促进农业发展、实现乡村人口减贫是老挝政府多年以来孜孜以求的发展目标。作为深植于老挝多年的亚钾国际，在注重企业发展的同时，也高度关注老挝乡村发展和农村减贫，多年来借鉴中国减贫做法和经验，通过促进老挝现代农业发展、实施产业扶贫项目、搭建农业技术培训平台、投资当地基础设施建设等多种措施助力老挝乡村发展，取得了很好的效果，受到了老挝方高度肯定和赞扬。

二、主要做法

一是引进新品种新技术新模式，促进现代农业发展。农业是老挝经济的重要支柱，水稻和蔬菜是老挝最主要的农作物，水稻种植面积占全国农作物种植面积的85%。全国超过70%的居民只种植一季水稻，种植技术落后导致水稻单产低，亩产只有200~300千克，很多农民温饱问题还没有解决。但老挝资源丰富，降水和热量充足，自然条件非常适合发展农业。针对这种状况，亚钾国际引进国内水稻种植技术和杂交水稻品种，在老挝占巴塞省孔县开发110公顷的三季稻种植示范基地，配套水利工程开发1200公顷。在管理上，采取大面积水稻集中式生产管理，并与国内水稻种植专业团队合作，将优良水稻品种、优质高产多季稻种植技术、现代农机装备引入老挝。亚钾国际采购自动化大型联合收割机，利用大型无人机开展播种、施肥、喷洒农药等工作，极大地提高了生产效率。在发展模式上，亚钾国际建立了"生态＋产业"发展模式，依托生态资源优势，以"稻渔生态＋循环种养"新模式为引领，探索试验多季稻种植，建立"稻渔共生"系统，打造标准化稻渔综合种养殖示范基地，实现"一田双收、稻渔双赢"的生态发展目标。

公司还向农民赠送钾肥，推广科学施肥技术，助力村民提产增收。

亚钾国际现代农业开发项目启动仪式

二是实施产业扶贫项目，推动当地村民减贫脱贫。推动土地流转，促进规模化种植。亚钾国际引导甘蒙省尕本村农民进行自愿流转土地，实行集中连片，统一种植，促进土地的集约化、规模化和现代化经营，提高土地利用效率和农民收入水平。建设蔬菜大棚。亚钾国际根据当地气候条件，在甘蒙省尕本村投资56万元，建起了45栋蔬菜大棚，引进了国外各种新、奇、特的蔬菜品种，发展特色经济作物。建设畜禽养殖示范场。为支持当地养殖业发展，亚钾国际引入了云南西双版纳畜禽科技有限公司，建立了畜禽养殖场，以养殖肉鸡为主，年肉鸡出栏14.4万只。农户生产的蔬菜和畜禽产品全部由公司收购，统一销售给公司矿区食堂。

三是搭建技术培训平台，为当地培育农业技术人才。"授人以鱼不如授人以渔"，亚钾国际多举措、多方式搭建农业技术合作、示范推广、人员培训平台，开展农业技术人才培训，为老挝培育专业技术人才，努力提高当地村民生产技能，带动老挝当地百姓脱贫致富。亚钾国际现代农业项目团队相继派出多名农业技术人员入驻老挝，实地调研、科学分析，依托现代农业多季稻、多季蔬菜实验基地，开展水稻苗期分级淹灌多季稻技术研究与示范，手把手教老挝农民种植水稻和蔬菜。此外，公司在甘蒙省尕本村举办蔬菜种植技术培训班9次，多个村民学会了蔬菜种植技术。其中，有18户农民在自己家房前屋后种上了小菜园，增加了村民收入。

四是广辟就业渠道，增加村民就业机会。对村里失地农户和有劳动能力的农民，亚钾国际通过认真研究，根据不同情况分别开辟了矿区公司就业，大棚蔬菜地、多季种植示范地工作等途径，最大限度增加村民就业机会。以重点扶贫村甘蒙省尕本村为例，安排到矿区工厂工作21人，安排到大棚蔬菜地工作15人，安排到多季农作物种植示范地工作26人，共安置村民62人，占总户数的64%。

五是热心公益项目，助力乡村振兴。在公共基础设施方面，亚钾国际帮助当地村庄建设发展，修建了中老亚钾友谊大桥，改善了当地居民的出行条件。在教育方面，公司投入资金修建了中老亚钾希望小学，推动教育事业发展。在医疗卫生方面，公司对有病的贫困户安排基本卫生保障，帮助村民普及医疗卫生知识，建立了备有药箱的卫生服务站。在社会文化方面，亚钾国际在扶贫村建立了老挝少数民族玛龚族文化活动中心，增设阅读室，配备了适合小学生、中学生阅读的各种类型的图书，解决贫困村孩子读书难问题。

三、成效与展望

一是提高了当地居民收入。亚钾国际通过发展多季农作物种植，显著提高了当地农民收入。原来种植一季作物时，农民每公顷收入仅为4600元，亚钾国际引入多季农作物种植后，农民每公顷保底收入

13800多元，增加了两倍以上。此外，亚钾国际高度重视本土化发展，多途径给当地人提供就业机会。当地村民不仅享受到先进农业带来的福利，农闲时期还能到厂里打工。目前企业已带动整体就业人数约12000人，其中带动老挝当地就业人数约8000人，有效促进了老挝当地经济发展和收入增长。

亚钾国际郭柏春董事长与援建小学的老挝小学生握手

二是提升了老挝农业竞争力。亚钾国际以种植环节的农业机械化和标准化为牵引，构建一套适应老挝的水稻全程机械化、现代化种植新模式。同时将中国水稻质量标准和种植技术推广到老挝各个省份，帮助老挝建立育种、种植、加工、出口等多季稻产业链，助推老挝水稻生产由传统农业向现代农业转变。在生产设备上，亚钾国际把中国制造植保无人机播种、施肥及防虫害技术引入老挝，助推其改进传统的水稻种植模式，助力老挝农业向高效、经济、可持续转型。

三是改善了当地基础设施条件。中老亚钾友谊大桥的建成通车，有效缓解了贫困村以及周边村庄多年的出行难问题，改善了当地交通条件。中老亚钾希望小学的建成，解决了全村和附近村庄孩子们就学难问题。卫生服务站的建设，缓解了当地村民看病难问题。

四是创出了可复制、可推广的"亚钾扶贫模式"。 亚钾国际产业扶贫项目，真正改变了老挝当地传统农业思维模式和理念，突出科技引领，强化融合发展，满足了村民对美好生活的向往。公司在产业扶贫项目中为当地建设蔬菜大棚，年产蔬菜可创收约12亿基普。老挝国家领导人及甘蒙省政府领导，多次到扶贫村莅临视察指导，并给予了高度赞赏与评价。公司的产业扶贫项目，被所在地区他曲政府树立为"产业扶贫典范企业"。

未来，亚钾国际将继续关注老挝乡村发展和乡村减贫，不断加大投入力度，把中国减贫经验和减贫模式持续传播到老挝，同老挝政府一起，为老挝农业和乡村发展贡献力量。

6

金融活水助力企业乘风破浪"走出去"

——金融机构支持企业开展国际合作

金融活水助力企业乘风破浪"走出去"
——金融机构支持企业开展国际合作

响应"一带一路"倡议，近年来，越来越多的企业实施"走出去"战略，而企业在开展国际合作时，通常面临大量的资金需求和风险挑战，单纯依靠企业自身力量在国际市场上拓展业务，难度较大。践行金融支持农业产业国际化发展要求，以中国农业银行、中国建设银行为代表的金融机构，大力创新工作思路，开发金融产品，在促进农业涉外企业开展国际合作方面发挥积极作用。

一、基本情况

我国企业在实施"走出去"战略中普遍面临融资渠道狭窄、融资难、融资贵的困境。境外企业由于处于新设起步阶段，资信及担保方面往往难以达到国外银行融资条件，因而，其流动资金和投资资金需求只能依靠境内企业的后续融资满足。目前，以金融机构借款为主的间接融资仍是企业"走出去"融资的主渠道，而实际却存在直接和间接资金支持、出口信用贷款严重不足等问题，同时，境外企业的资金需求主要通过投资主体内保外贷方式满足，而内保外贷审批手续烦琐，融资成本较高。我国橡胶企业广东省广垦橡胶集团有限公司（以下简称"广垦橡胶"）及海南天然橡胶产业集团股份有限公司（以下简称"海南橡胶"）的国际开拓中即存在上述融资诉求。以中国农业银行、中国建设银行为代表的金融机构在解决相关企业金融诉求方面积极作为，为企业的海外合作提供了充分支持。

广垦橡胶是成立于2002年的天然橡胶种植、加工、销售企业，年产优质橡胶种苗200万株，在国内拥有天然橡胶种植面积65万亩，年产天然橡胶20多万吨，是中国三大天然橡胶生产基地之一，具备丰厚资质和良好发展前景。这些年，广垦橡胶积极实施海外发展战略，扩大生产规模，在泰国、马来西亚、印度尼西亚、新加坡等地建立了大型橡胶加工厂、生产基地和贸易公司，目前已拥有17家海外子公司。随着集团生产经营规模不断扩大，企业海外子公司的地位以及作用越发重要，维持海外子公司生产经营稳定、流动资金充足成为集团的重要工作之一。

广垦橡胶海外工厂全景图

广垦橡胶看中新加坡的经济和地理优势，在新加坡成立子公司，负责开展日常生产销售工作，并进行海外融资、扩大生产规模。新加坡子公司处于扩张时期，需要大量资金投入建设，而集团合作的上下游客户多为知名企业，货款结算周期有固定的节奏，资金回笼速度赶不上扩张所需资金支出需要。另外，海外子公司新一批天然橡胶采购需求已接近付款期限，需按时对外支付货款，由于前期回笼资金大部分已用于企业扩大生产，加之国内集团无法及时调拨支援，导致新加坡子公司资金一时无法周转。广垦橡胶新加坡子公司成立时间较短，若在境外银行申请授信需较长时间且不确定因素较多，短期内无法从海外直接获得融资。企业面临违约赔偿风险，急需金融机构提供资金支持。

中国建设银行与海南天然橡胶产业集团股份有限公司召开座谈会

海南天然橡胶产业集团股份有限公司在"走出去"过程中也存在跨境金融资金与服务支持的诉求。作为国内最大的天然橡胶生产企业，近年来，海南橡胶以国家"一带一路"倡议为契机，加强与橡胶主产国的合作、建立长期战略关系，在印度尼西亚、喀麦隆等地建立橡胶生产基地，通过并购壮大企业生产规模。为了扩大在"一带一路"沿线国家和地区的橡胶生产基地建设，同时推进橡胶的国际贸易，海南橡胶于 2022 年跨境收购新加坡境内 Halcyon Agri Corporation Limited

（以下简称"HAC 公司"或标的公司）的部分已发行普通股股份（约占 HAC 公司已发行普通股股份的 36%）。本次收购意义重大，能够有效扩大产业版图、提高企业在行业内及国际上的影响力和竞争力。但是收购过程中，急需银行提供内保外贷、信用证、国际商业转贷款、跨境融资性风险参与、跨境直贷通等融资服务。

二、主要做法

以中国农业银行、中国建设银行为代表的金融机构，在金融支持农业企业海外投资合作过程中，充分考虑主体实际诉求，为主体提供适合的金融产品和融资方案，同时优化内部审核管理流程，加快融资办理流程，高效解决"走出去"企业在境外扩大再生产中遇到的"急难愁盼"问题，为企业发展保驾护航。

一是量体裁衣，制定稳妥快速融资方案。在广垦橡胶的案例中，中国农业银行通过对客户交易背景进行分析，结合中国农业银行海外分行布局情况，向客户推介了内保外贷产品方案，由中国农业银行境内分行开出以广垦橡胶为保函申请人，中国农业银行新加坡分行为保函受益人的融资性保函，由中国农业银行新加坡分行为广垦橡胶新加坡子公司提供短期贷款。在海南橡胶的案例中，中国建设银行充分考虑到跨境并购存在不确定因素多、资金需求时效性强的特征，将海南橡胶海外并购融资确定为重点事项，特事特办，避免错失并购机会。

二是优化流程，提高融资审批效率。在广垦橡胶的案例中，由于企业内部对开户管理要求严格，融资时效性要求强，G 集团提出当自有资金充足时希望随时还款。了解到上述需求后，中国农业银行认真梳理流程，寻求上级行协助，广东省分支行多层联动，与新加坡分行紧密联系，节省企业开户时间，项目从启动到落地不到 20 天，为企业生产经营提供了及时的金融支持，缓解了企业短期资金压力，帮助企业规避违约赔偿风险。在海南橡胶的案例中，根据企业融资需求，中国建设银行进行总分行联动，成立专项工作团队、快速响应，方案敲定后，迅速撰写授信申报材料，内外联动，几天内迅速完成《跨境并购贷款尽职调查与风险评估报告》，并顺利通过评审小组的评估，上报总行审批部。

三、成效及展望

一是助力企业发展，不断提升国际竞争力。在中国农业银行资金支持下，广垦橡胶境外企业渡过难关，资金回流稳定充裕，顺利扩大市场份额。近几年，广垦橡胶无资金短缺的后顾之忧，一心一意提升产品品质，优化产品结构，提高品牌国际知名度，80%以上的产品供给全球百强轮胎企业，其产品在航空航天等国防领域的应用比例不断提高，逐渐占领国内主要高端市场。在中国建设银行的支持下，海南橡胶通过协议转让和强制要约合计收购 HAC 公司约 10.86 亿股股份（占 HAC 已发行普通股股份的 68.1%）。并购 HAC 公司后，海南橡胶迅速获取天然橡胶及乳胶的海外加工产能，进一步提升了海南橡胶在天然橡胶国际市场的话语权及影响力，帮助海南橡胶获得标的公司下游客户资源，并利用标的公司的欧美贸易网络进一步融入全球天然橡胶贸易体系。在金融支撑背景下，"走出去"橡胶企业在海外逐渐发展壮大，在带动当地产业发展的同时，将企业发展成果融入当地经济社会发展，积极开展国际公益事业，在解决当地就业、资助农工孩子上学等方面发挥积极作用，树立起良好的企业国际合作形象、提升国际影响力。

二是丰富了金融支持农业对外合作的经验模式。中国农业银行在支持广垦橡胶过程中，全方位、多渠道了解了涉外企业经营情况、发展动向和资金需求，强化了专业化服务水平，目前已经建立起省分支行三级联动专业营销团队，为客户提供政策咨询、汇率分析等差异化服务，立足客户需求，不断提升服务意识和服务水平。中国建设银行通过海南橡胶并购业务，了解了涉外企业需求，熟悉了涉外企业贷款融资流程和要求，建立了对涉外企业贷款融资项目前景分析判断方法，开发了对涉外企业贷款融资的金融产品。目前，中国建设银行通过国际商业转贷款、跨境融资通等产品，支持涉农企业放眼国际，在国际市场做大做强。中国建设银行还通过跨境退税贷、信保贷、出口贷等为小微优质涉农出口企业提供全线上、纯信用的跨境快贷，解决小微出口企业融资贵、融资难问题。同时，中国建设银行还加强与涉农企业全产业链合作，针对自由贸易试验区、综合保税区、跨境经济合作试验区提供中国建设银行"全球撮合家"金融服务平台。

三是提高金融服务农业外交大局的使命担当。中国农业银行利用发达的全球体系资源，"一点接入，全球响应"，发挥综合金融和"三农"服务优势，用好"表内+表外""境内+境外""商行+投行""线下+线上"的全资产业服务体系，拓宽跨国集团企业融资渠道，加大国际金融供给，全方位支持企业放心"出海"，精准高效服务好实体经济，以更加优质的跨境金融服务，满足企业高质量发展需求，为践行"一带一路"倡议作出金融贡献。中国建设银行贯彻落实"进一步增强服务国家建设能力、防范金融风险能力、参与国际竞争能力"三个能力建设，充分发挥综合化经营、集成化服务优势，内外联动，总分联动，丰富涉农企业并购贷款、融资租赁、公司信用类债务融资工具（包括短期融资券、中期票据、资产支持票据、乡村振兴票据等），不断降本增效，为企业综合竞争力和行业高质量发展注入新活力。

未来，相关金融机构将进一步落实"优化进出口贸易和对外投资金融服务，强化国际合作，支持有实力有意愿的农业企业'走出去'"的具体要求，加强产品创新力度，优化审批流程，为我国农业企业的国际化发展提供金融保障。

7

探索"粮食安全"供应链新模式

——爱菊中哈粮油合作项目

探索"粮食安全"供应链新模式
——爱菊中哈粮油合作项目

粮食安全是"国之大者"。2016年，爱菊集团积极践行国家"一带一路"倡议，走出国门在哈萨克斯坦建立北哈州农产品物流加工园区，通过构建国内国际优质粮食"双循环"大通道，探索发展了"一带一路"粮食安全供应链服务新模式，为中哈两国友好往来树立了典范。

一、基本情况

西安爱菊粮油工业集团有限公司，其前身为西安华峰面粉厂，始建于1934年，是一家老字号粮油企业，现为国家级农业产业化重点龙头企业、全国供应链创新与应用示范企业。"优质的粮食源地"一直是爱菊集团关注的重点。哈萨克斯坦富营养的黑土地深达1.5米，自然条件好，但粮食亩产150~200斤，远低于美国和中国的亩产，是人类绿色、有机农产品的净土之一，具有较好的发展前景。2015年，集团积极响应国家"一带一路"倡议，经过反复调研和多方考量，最终将哈萨克斯坦确定为新的粮源基地。2015年12月，在中哈两国领导的见证下，爱菊集团与哈萨克斯坦政府签署了"对哈投资合作协议"。2016年5月，爱菊集团开始建立北哈州农产品物流加工园区，园区占地5000亩，计划投资20亿元，分五大板块，包括粮油生产收储与食品加工板块、牛羊养殖与牛羊肉加工、乡村旅游板块、产业技术服务板块、中国商品展销馆。目前已投资约 2 亿元，建成年加工 30 万吨的油脂厂 1 个，合计仓容 15 万吨的粮库 2 个，配备年物流能力 50 万吨的铁路专用线 4 条，推广小麦、油菜籽、葵花籽"订单农业"种植 150 万亩，建成日处理 1000 吨的烘干塔、日处理 500 吨的油脂浸出车间 2 个。目前，爱菊集团北哈州农产品物流加工园区是"中哈产能投资与合作清单"中唯一的农业加工型粮食项目，受到哈萨克斯坦各级政府的高度关注与支持。目前，已获得当地补贴 3200 万元，获得当地银行低息贷款折合人民币 8000 万元。

二、主要做法

爱菊集团积极践行国家"一带一路"倡议，构建国内国际优质粮食"双循环"大通道，建成"北哈州、阿拉山口、西安"三位一体跨国大物流、大加工的全产业链"闭环"供应链体系，打通了我国与"一带一路"沿线国家特别是中亚国家的物流供应链，探索发展了"一带一路"粮食安全供应链服务新模式。

一是探路创先河，树"爱菊"中哈新形象。克服冬日寒冷，仅用时半年，爱菊集团就建成哈萨克斯坦最大的油脂厂——哈萨克斯坦爱菊农产品物流加工园区一期年加工 30 万吨油脂厂，创造哈萨克斯坦基础建设中的一个奇迹，树立了中国企业的良好形象。历时半年，实现"中欧货运班列"首趟满载货物回程。进口哈萨克斯坦非转基因优质油脂约 2000 吨，扩大企业影响力，受到社会各界和中哈两国政府的关注。

二是创新理念，构建"三位一体"跨国大物流、大加工全产业供应链体系。爱菊集团目前已建成以北哈州爱菊农产品物流加工园区为境外物流加工基地、新疆阿拉山口农产品物流加工爱菊园区为"境内关外"中转分拨中心、西安国际港务区爱菊农产品物流加工园区为集散中心的三位一体优质粮食大物流、大加工体系，旨在打造有效的欧亚海外粮仓，让粮食"买得到、运得回"。其中，爱菊集团北哈州农产品物流加工园区为"境外前沿产地枢纽"，主要侧重功能为"原料生产和初加工"，内可辐射北哈州乃至周边数百公里其他州，外可连接西伯利亚平原优质农产品产地，进口俄罗斯、乌克兰等周边国家的优质小麦、油菜籽等原料。爱菊集团阿拉山口农产品物流加工园区为"境内中转集散枢纽"，主要侧重功能为"精深加工和分拨中转"，具有"境内关外"这一特殊性，为连接中外的关键节点。外可直接连接爱菊集团北哈州农产品物流加工园区，内可直接连接全国各大城市，并可连接爱菊集团西安国际港务区农产品物流加工园区。爱菊集团西安农产品物流加工园区为"境内集散枢纽"，主要侧重功能为"集散辐射"，位于全国唯一内陆港"西安国际港务区"，是"一带一路"的桥头堡，是西北枢纽龙头，以此为中心，辐射西北、面向全国。

爱菊集团在哈萨克斯坦的农产品物流加工园区

三是创新机制，组建新型订单农业合作社。爱菊集团初期在哈萨克斯坦租地进行粮食种植时，受西方舆论的恶意攻击，当地农场主抵触情绪大，进展不顺利。针对这种情况，同时考虑到哈萨克斯坦"种粮难、卖粮难"这一突出问题，爱菊集团开始推行"政府＋银行＋企业＋农场主＋高校"的新型订单农业合作模式，组建新型订单农业合作社。联合西北农林科技大学、哈萨克斯坦国立大学、当地农场主等共同参与，采取"订单农业、订单收购"方式，实施种子研发、种植、管理、收割、收购、存储一条龙运营策略，指导当地农户"种什么、种多少"，解决了当地"卖粮难"的问题。通过"预付货款"的方式，解决了当地农场主的种粮费用问题。爱菊集团新型订单农业合作模式打造了一个产业闭环，即爱菊集团预付银行订单货款、银行给予农户贷款、政府给予银行借款贴息、政府给予农户种植补贴、政府给予企业出口补贴。该模式实现了多方共赢，受到哈萨克斯坦社会的一致欢迎，逐步建立了中外农商互联农产品跨国供应链，确保了国内长期稳定的优质粮源供给，也进一步增加了哈萨克斯坦人民对中国的好感。

四是创新模式，"抱团出海"共赢发展。 爱菊集团致力于将哈萨克斯坦爱菊园区打造为我国境外投资平台，吸引更多中国企业入区建厂，进而形成产业集群。目前杨凌农业自贸区拟与爱菊集团合作，共建海外园区，将哈萨克斯坦爱菊园区打造为国家级农业园区。本园区计划由粮油生产收储与食品加工、牛羊养殖与牛羊肉加工、产业技术服务、中亚民俗文化与乡村旅游和智慧园区服务中心五大板块组成。目前，已有十多家中国企业与集团进行了初步沟通，有意愿入驻哈萨克斯坦爱菊园区。

五是创新管理，变"走出去"为"融进去"。 爱菊集团注重本土化经营。哈萨克斯坦园区主要员工均为当地人民，同时根据当地风俗习惯优化管理方式，主要包括适度增加工人工资；增加各种奖励，如出勤奖励等；及时发放日常工资和当天发放加班工资；举办各种聚会活动，加强当地员工对中国人的好感；邀请当地骨干员工赴中国西安参观学

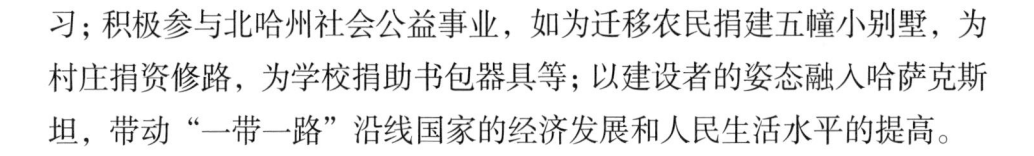

习；积极参与北哈州社会公益事业，如为迁移农民捐建五幢小别墅，为村庄捐资修路，为学校捐助书包器具等；以建设者的姿态融入哈萨克斯坦，带动"一带一路"沿线国家的经济发展和人民生活水平的提高。

三、成效及展望

经过近 8 年的探索和发展，爱菊集团哈萨克斯坦农产品物流加工园区建设取得显著成效，境外园区产值不断提升，农业产业链条逐步完善。目前，爱菊集团在哈萨克斯坦建立优质粮食订单种植基地 150 万亩。2015 年以来累计向国内输入非转基因优质油脂、优质面粉、有机小麦等 30 余万吨，极大提升了爱菊粮油的品质。通过打造"三位一体"跨国供应链，爱菊集团增加了优质粮食、优质食品供给。近年来，爱菊集团平均年粮油销量增加 5%，平均增加收入 2000 万元。据初步品牌评估，爱菊的品牌价值在 2 亿元以上。爱菊产品受到了国家、省、市各级领导的欢迎与肯定。"订单农业"模式为哈萨克斯坦"农业多赢"探索出一条新路，受到了当地各方的一致好评。2018 年 8 月 17 日，哈萨克斯坦首任总统纳扎尔巴耶夫乘专机莅临视察，表示"该项目是中哈产能投资与合作的典范"，给予了充分肯定。2023 年"爱菊粮油'一带一路'农产品供应链服务模式"入选国家首批新型消费发展典型案例。

哈萨克斯坦不仅是中亚地区的重要国家，还是中国"一带一路"倡议向西延伸的第一站。经过多年艰苦探索，爱菊集团在哈萨克斯坦交出了一份优异成绩单，也使得爱菊粮油成为中国农产品市场上一张亮丽的"名片"。未来，爱菊集团将继续加大投资力度，加强与哈萨克斯坦农场主的合作，深入推进中哈农业产能合作，实现共赢发展。

8

共建防灾减灾体系，携手保护生态环境

——中哈农业旱灾与虫灾监测预警项目

共建防灾减灾体系，携手保护生态环境
——中哈农业旱灾与虫灾监测预警项目

哈萨克斯坦粮食作物管理水平不高，灾害严重，产量很不稳定。为解决该问题中哈双方研究团队进行了相关合作，旨在利用中方在大数据挖掘和应用服务方面的技术优势和成熟经验，由哈方合作单位收集和整理哈国农业有关方面的历史数据，中方团队结合农业"空天地"一体化监测网络的建设，在数据分析和模型研发的基础上，自主研发农业灾害监测与预警系统平台，对于开展当地粮食作物灾害检测水平、提升我国先进技术在"一带一路"沿线国家应用具有重要意义。

一、基本情况

哈萨克斯坦耕地面积有 3 亿亩，是世界最大的小麦面粉出口国和第六大粮食出口国，在中国粮食进口中排名第三位，是我国中亚粮食与畜产品后备基地。2019 年 12 月，哈萨克斯坦总统到中亚生态与环境研究中心建设的中哈农业大数据分析中心视察，提出要将遥感大数据技术推广应用到哈萨克斯坦全国，中国驻哈大使馆高度重视，将其作为中哈科技合作的重点方向。针对哈国农业灾害以及对地观测技术的合作需求，中方团队与哈萨克斯坦赛福林农业技术大学、哈萨克斯坦农业科学院土壤与农业化学研究所联合开展了干旱和病虫害对地监测和预警研究工作，已建成小麦监测示范区 3 处，设立国产农业气象站及虫情监测地面站。中方团队基于国产高分影像数据和深度学习模型提取了哈国北部三州田块数据，基于干旱监测提出小麦估产方法。同时中方团队自主研发农业灾害监测系统平台一套，集成了地面监测、虫情识别、农情信息提取、干旱及病虫害预警，开发了野外土地利用及病虫害调查APP，为哈萨克斯坦农业自然灾害的防治提供软硬件支撑示范平台。

该项目一方面通过开展哈萨克斯坦粮食作物灾害监测和预警系统研发和示范，帮助哈方提高粮食作物灾害监测能力和水平；另一方面推进了我国遥感卫星和北斗定位系统及大数据、云计算等信息技术在中亚国家农业中的服务与应用。2023年度中哈团队成功召开"一带一路"可持续发展与自然灾害监测国际研讨会，并举办了"一带一路"国家农业灾害遥感智能化监测及管理国际培训班，获得了学员的一致好评，为哈方合作单位培养相关技术人才20余名。

二、主要做法

中哈双方各自依托本国科学院支持，通过优势互补的合作模式开展项目研发和农业项目落地实施。其中，中方优势在于遥感农业监测、智慧农业信息化及设备研发，哈方优势在于传统地面监测、无人机及实地研究。最终通过合作的"空天地"一体化监测开展大范围农业旱灾病虫害监测及预警研究。

项目实施本着求同存异以及互相尊重的原则，不断磨合和调整工作模式，充分利用当前便捷的网络技术推进项目顺利实施。特别是2019年冬天以来，在新冠肺炎疫情影响了实际人员往来和交流的情况下，中哈双方共建联合研究创新合作范式，具体合作机制如下：

一是建立院级组织协调机制。在推动国际合作基础上，基于项目具体实施单位，建立了双方院长级别交流机制。其中，中方由中国科学院深圳先进技术研究院、中国科学院中亚生态与环境研究中心领导，哈方由国立科学院土壤所所长、大学校长等共同组建合作项目工作专班，负责统筹项目的具体开展、人员交流等管理协调工作。

二是建立数据共享机制。依托"中哈农业大数据中心"，合作建立了"空天地"数据共享机制。其中，当地的地面采集数据优先保留在合作方本国，通过大数据中心云平台与我方共享，而遥感相关原始数据保留在国内，通过研发灾害监测系统模型的实地部署方式，对境外提供成果数据共享服务。

三是建立有效沟通和人员互访交流机制。在院级组织协调机制基础上，制定了人员定期交流互访机制，便于双方人员的科技能力提升和实地部署。疫情防控期间，主要采用线上交流及线上培训方式，实现了有效的沟通和项目进度推进。疫情过后，已成功组织哈方人员来华参加培训，并组织中方人员回访开展实验区调研和项目交流。

四是建立明确工作任务负责制。在国家数据安全规范下，双方各自侧重及互相配合以开展项目工作内容。在长期合作交流机制下双方明确了工作任务，完成了地面监测设备的对接以及部分历史灾害数据的收集等工作。例如，中方团队前往哈方合作单位试验田考察，沿途收集到春小麦、春玉米、豌豆、亚麻、土豆、油葵等多种作物样点300余个，为地面监测提供了大量基础数据。中方团队跟随哈萨克斯坦农业科学院植物保护和生物检疫中心蝗虫防治研究团队，开展蝗虫过境之后的爆发考察，收集到阿拉木图州面积约为1公顷的蝗虫源地1块，根据实际情况提出了多个方面的合作内容：蝗虫和其他物体的地面防护数据收集；遥感、卫星数据识别与制图；现场传感器实施、测试；软件的开发；无人机相关的项目，传感器研发；教育、实习及实践；干旱和盐渍化对农业产量影响；积雪厚度制图；作物模型与遥感数据同化等。

三、成效及展望

一是完成哈萨克斯坦北部三州和南部锡尔河流域耕地地块提取。锡尔河矢量总面积约为 63410 平方千米，实际耕地面积约为 34556 平方千米，锡尔河总耕地矢量图文件大小为 67 兆字节，锡尔河总计有 339565 块面数。哈萨克斯坦北部三州包括：科斯塔奈州、北哈萨克斯坦州和阿克莫拉州，提取耕地总面积为 20925 平方千米，北部总耕地矢量图文件大小为 9.9 兆字节，北部三州总计有 59210 块面数。

二是帮助哈方收集了大量气象数据资料。依托本项目建成地面监测站点 3 处，覆盖面积达 2 万公顷。其中，中国境内 1 处，位于新疆奇台县国家粮食生产基地，包含农业气象站 1 套，监测内容涉及降雨量、空气温湿度、大气气压、辐射总量、土壤墒情等内容；虫情测报灯 1 台，且以上设备均正常运行。哈国境内 2 处，包含农业气象站 2 套和虫情测报灯 2 台。目前，哈方合作单位接收气象数据累计 1 万余条，虫害照片达千余张。

三是帮助哈方建立了覆盖全哈萨克斯坦的农业旱灾监测系统。我方为哈方合作单位开发虫情测报和农业气象站数据接收系统 1 套，目前已在当地部署完毕，能够正常开展在线监测和调试、气象干旱监测、虫情识别和统计等。为哈方合作单位开发基于遥感的农业旱灾监测系统 1 套，目前已部署于哈方当地，通过长时序遥感观测，采用了基于植被—温度、作物健康指数等多种气象和土壤干旱指标，针对作物干旱做到覆盖全哈萨克斯坦地区每 8 天一期的观测预报。

四是构建了中亚农业及社会经济数据库。团队整理收集中亚农业及社会经济数据，编写各种文档处理小程序，实现自动翻译功能。整理原始文件夹 1 万多个，文件 10 万多个，文本将近 40 万条记录，建立了一套可检索的中亚农业及社会经济数据库，并公开于全网以供研究人员浏览查询，是目前中国第一套可查询检索的中亚农业及社会经济数据库，该数据库还提供专业的数据聚合工具。

五是通过举办会议、人员培训等扩大了项目的影响力。双方合作召开"一带一路"可持续发展与自然灾害监测国际研讨会，并举办了"一带一路"国家农业灾害遥感智能化监测及管理国际培训班。中方研究团队就农业干旱监测和小麦估产等方面，对哈方技术人员开展了遥感影像处理技术和干旱监测技术的培训，共培养哈国技术人员30余名。此次培训得到了国内外媒体的广泛关注，产生了良好的国际影响。

中方团队与哈萨克斯坦研究人员开展讨论会

针对项目后期合作发展态势，对于中亚农情监测与数据挖掘、管理、发布平台的建设要求长期持续投入。开展农业大数据系统的应用示范只是个开端与起步，加强对中亚地区农情监测及粮食作物灾害监测工作，提高监测产品的时空精度，继续收集整理中亚的农业及社会经济数据，服务于后期的数据挖掘工作，对于中亚及国家安全稳定意义重大。后期研究团队将以哈萨克斯坦作为示范样板，向整个中亚以及其他"丝绸之路"沿线国家推广数字农业产品及应用，同时带动我国企业的监测设备发展，提高我国在中亚的科技号召力。

9

技术引领，构建人类命运共同体

——菌草技术援外实践

技术引领，构建人类命运共同体
——菌草技术援外实践

菌草技术是由我国完全拥有知识产权的原创技术，涵盖以草代木栽培食用菌、生态治理、菌草及菌物饲料、生物质能源与材料开发等领域。自1994年起，菌草技术被列入我国对外援助项目，现已传播到106个国家。长期以来，依托菌草技术，我国援外专家服务国家总体外交大局，积极对接"一带一路"倡议，为构建更加紧密的人类命运共同体作出了积极贡献。

一、基本情况

自然资源稀少，经济基础薄弱，自然灾害频发、水土流失和土地退化严重，这是"一带一路"沿线许多国家普遍面临的发展难题。菌草技术作为有效的"扶贫草"，实现了光、热、水三大农业资源综合高效利用，能够实现植物、动物、菌物三物循环生产，有利于生态、粮食、能源安全。而且菌草技术投资小，能够在短期内实现经济、社会、环境三大效益结合，非常适合在自然资源贫瘠、经济基础薄弱的地方发展，因此，菌草技术在20世纪就被我国列为重点援外技术。经过几十年的努力，尤其在"一带一路"倡议的推动下，菌草技术合作已经成为中国与全球各国携手，共同应对环境恶化和贫穷，增加全球人民福祉的生动实践。

二、主要做法

为有效在受援国进行示范和推广，中国菌草技术援外专家组根据各受援国的实际需求和现有生产技术水平，从增强当地发展新兴菌草业提升自主发展能力出发，全面示范结合水土保持、土壤改良、饲料加工、食用菌生产与加工的菌草产业链，为增加就业、消除贫困提供新途径。在示范与推广模式上，菌草对外援助专家组与当地农业部门的推广体系相结合，形成较为完整的菌草技术推广体系，形成"四结合"和"五化"措施，摸索出"基地+旗舰点+农户"推广模式。具体如下：

一是坚持"四结合"和"五化"措施。"四结合"，即与当地自然条件相结合、与当地政府相结合、与当地群众相结合、与当地需求相结合。"五化"，即技术本土化、操作简便化、生产标准化、产业系统化、农户组织化。例如，在莱索托，在制定推广菌草平菇栽培模式时专家组充分考虑到莱气候干燥这一自然条件，采取半脱袋覆土栽培模式。制定各项技术指标和操作规范，做到直观化、数字化、简便化，使莱工人、农民"一看就懂、一学就会、一做就成"。同时建立了各种网络交流群，包括菌草种植生产群、菌草菇栽培群、菌草菇栽培袋生产群等，援外专家组实时在线提供指导，促进当地农户相互学习、共同进步，加速中国援助菌草技术顺利进村入户，提高当地民众自身发展能力，促进脱贫致富，带动当地新兴产业发展，保护生态环境良性发展。

二是实施"基地+旗舰点+农户"推广模式。在斐济、南非、卢旺达和巴布亚新几内亚等国摸索出"基地+旗舰点+农户"的推广模式。专家组按照不同的培训对象，将培训分为三个层次。

第一个层次是培训有一定基础知识的、负责当地各项农业技术宣传和推广的专业技术人员，包括农业科研人员、农业部和各区农业技术负责人，希望他们能快速掌握所学知识并能实现快速传播和推广。

专家组不仅在基地和区农业站或示范点进行现场培训，还在旗舰点里建立田间学校，从选择栽培场地、建菇棚，到如何保温、降温、保湿、防风、控光线等创造菌草菇生长最佳环境进行手把手教学，然后学员再指导各区农户进行菌草生产。

第二个层次是培训当地各项农业技术带头人和骨干，包括各示范点的骨干和社区骨干、合作社负责人、重点示范户，以及农业院校的学生。首先指导学员进行生产栽培，在生产过程中查找问题、发现问题、解决问题；其次从理论上进行区域性集中培训，使学员们牢固掌握菌草菇高产栽培标准化生产技术，并能自主解决生产中遇到的问题。

第三个层次是培训拟从事菌草技术生产的新农户。采取感受型学习模式，通过农业部、合作社、协会等团体负责人召集学员进行区域性分批分次集中学习培训，专家组带领学员参观基地、品尝菌草菇，激发学员们对菌草技术的兴趣，再进行理论授课，最后让学员进行体验式生产实践，使学员了解菌草技术并初步掌握基本技术要点，为后续从事菌草产业奠定良好基础。

中国菌草技术援外专家在中非共和国传播菌草技术

三、成效及展望

一是促进减贫，助力受援国农业可持续发展。菌草技术对外合作服务"一带一路"建设成效明显，对合作国群众脱贫致富，特别是对提高当地妇女地位和增加青少年就业起到了很好的促进作用，成为中国协助国际减贫的生动实践。据不完全统计，在非洲，菌草技术快速改变了当地菇类生产模式，菌种制作成本降低90%，产量比先前提高两倍以上，产品远销刚果（金）、乌干达、布隆迪等周边国家。有2万多个家庭（农户）通过菌草援助项目直接受益，改善了生活状况。菌草技术援外专家组和南非政府通过建立研究培训基地、菇农合作社旗舰点和菌草培育示范点，为农村地区失业人员提供了200多个固定工作岗位，1万多户家庭从中受益。菌草技术的传播使当地蘑菇从无到有，并走上了千家万户的餐桌，丰富了当地人民营养来源，为消除贫困作出重要贡献，被誉为"中南合作典范"。

中国菌草技术援外专家在莱索托传播菌草技术——当地农户喜获丰收

二是"授人以渔"，助力受援国科技产业发展。菌草对外合作项目为受援国农户提供大量培训，还为当地学校提供科教实践基地、开设"菌草课堂"，在当地大学举办菌草科学讲座开展长期的科教合作。在卢旺达，中国菌草技术专家在当地组织举办菌草技术培训班 57 期，培训当地学员 2064 人次，示范推广菌草生产农户超过 3500 多户；在巴布亚新几内亚，菌草技术已推广到 9 个省 17 个地区，累计培训 1984 人次，推广 12770 多农户，4 万多名民众受益，东部高地省把菌草作为发展经济、实现可持续发展目标的支柱产业。

三是深入人心，获得受援国高度认可。菌草技术为"一带一路"农业发展开辟了一条全新的道路，受到受援国政府和人民的高度评价。为表彰中国菌草专家为中非农业发展所作贡献，中非共和国总统图瓦德拉在首都班吉举行的 61 周年国庆庆典上，为 6 名中国援非菌草技术专家颁授国家感恩勋章。在斐济，菌草援助项目示范推广充分发挥菌草循环利用优势。种植菌草一举多得，既为菌菇栽培提供了充足原料，又有效缓解了当地牧场旱季青饲料匮乏的问题，促进了畜牧业发展，同时还为当地水土流失治理做出示范，受到斐济各界的一致好评。斐济农业部将"优化利用菌草提高畜牧业生产力"作为该国促进农业发展五项举措之一。2019 年 3 月 29 日，菌草技术被列入"中国—太平洋岛国农业部长会议"上发布的《楠迪宣言》中。

四是促进合作，助力国家外交大局。1994 年，菌草技术被列为"南南合作"项目和联合国开发计划署"中国与其他发展中国家优先合作项目"。1999 年菌草技术项目的成功实施在巴布亚新几内亚坚持"一个中国"的外交斗争中起到了积极作用，促进中国福建省与巴布亚新几内亚东部高地省结成友好省，时任福建省省长习近平签署友好省协议，并为菌草技术发明者林占熺研究员颁发"一等功"奖励。目前，菌草技术已经以培训、教育、合作与援助等方式传播至 106 个国家，其中包括许多"一带一路"沿线国家。2019 年 4 月 18 日，第 73 届联合国大会上，中国常驻联合国代表团与联合国经社事务部共同举办了题为"菌草技术：'一带一路'倡议促进落实联合国 2030 年可持续发展议程的实质性贡献"的高级别会议，本届联合国大会主席埃斯皮诺萨在会议上表示，菌草技术"为发展绿色经济树立了榜样，为当地青年和妇女创造了绿色就业的机会，是推动'一带一路'沿线国家农业合作的一项重要实践"。

下一步，围绕以菌草技术援外项目助力"一带一路"沿线国家农业可持续发展，继续加强菌草科学与技术研究，提升菌草技术援外效果。加强菌草技术国际传播能力建设，宣传菌草技术在发展农业、减贫脱困、生态保护、绿色发展等方面的重要作用，讲好"菌草佳话"，为增强中国与"一带一路"沿线国家友好合作贡献力量。

10

凝心聚力,打造中国援外技术品牌

——布隆迪高级农业专家技术援助项目

凝心聚力，打造中国援外技术品牌
——布隆迪高级农业专家技术援助项目

布隆迪位于非洲中东部，是典型的农业国家，农业人口占比接近90%。由于基础设施薄弱、农业技术落后等因素，布隆迪农业生产力较为低下，农产品不能自给自足，面临严重的粮食安全危机。为落实中非合作论坛北京峰会领导人有关承诺，中国农业农村部国际交流服务中心自2009年起连续承担五期援布隆迪高级农业专家组技术援助项目，有力促进了布隆迪水稻、畜牧等领域的快速发展，对推动中布双边顺利开展农业领域深度合作，打造更为紧密的中国—布隆迪命运共同体作出了重要贡献。

一、基本情况

布隆迪高级农业专家技术援助项目是在中非合作论坛框架下开展的技术援助项目。2006年11月，中非合作论坛北京峰会上通过了《中非合作论坛北京峰会宣言》和《中非合作论坛——北京行动计划（2007—2009年）》，中方承诺向非洲派遣100名高级农业技术专家，在非洲建立10个有特色的农业技术示范中心，加强与非洲在农业实用技术和农业人力资源开发方面的合作。为落实中非合作论坛北京峰会领导人有关承诺，中国政府分别于2009年8月、2012年5月、2015年11月、2018年3月、2020年3月向布隆迪派出5批共计48人次专家，农业农村部国际交流服务中心负责管理实施。援助领域主要涉及水稻、农产品加工、水产、果树、畜禽、土肥等。

援布隆迪农业专家杨华德与布隆迪人民分享水稻收获的喜悦

二、主要做法

布隆迪经济发展水平低、农业技术较为落后、农业技术推广能力较差。援布隆迪高级农业专家组秉持中非合作论坛北京峰会精神，攻坚克难、因地制宜，凭借其扎实的专业基础、踏实奉献的工作作风，探索发展了欠发达国家农业对外援助新路径和新模式。

一是创新模式，探索种植杂交水稻生产性投入基金模式。布隆迪地处非洲大陆东部，属热带气候，降水充沛，自然条件适合水稻生产。但由于当地水稻品种单产偏低，布隆迪饱受粮食短缺困扰。中国专家组深入田间地头调研试验，足迹遍布布隆迪15个水稻种植省份，成功挑选引进8种适合当地的稻种，解决了当地山区因稻瘟病减产甚至绝收的历史难题，并实现部分稻种本土化生产。在援助模式上，专家组进行了"建立杂交水稻示范生产投入基金，形成可持续发展机制"的探索，即为农户提供首季杂交水稻种植所需的种子、肥料、农药等费用作为"生产性投入基金"，并对种植户提供技术指导及技术培训。首季水稻收获后，农户自行售卖稻谷，并将其总收入中的生产成本（专家组提供的种子、肥料、农药等费用）自行上交至示范村合作社，合作社负责将本村农户上交的生产成本存入指定资金账户，作为下季生产投入，每个生产季按此循环，实现示范村水稻生产的可持续发展，真正实现"援助一个项目，发展一个产业，致富一方百姓"的目标，为改善当地民生发挥了积极作用。

二是创新机制，培养青年致富带头人和优秀农业人才。布隆迪农业领域人才匮乏，专业技术能力较弱，缺乏系统的专业知识。援布隆迪高级农业专家组始终将对布隆迪农牧业及环境部系统内官员、技术人员及农户培养作为核心工作任务，传授农业领域实用技术，传播先进农业发展理念，调动农民积极性。专家组定期对示范村农户进行技术培训，提高农民生产技能，鼓励村民之间相互交流技术、沟通信息、取长补短、共同致富。专家组精心制定农户增产增收、脱贫致富的可持续发展机制，选择文化基础较高，愿意服务乡亲、带领乡亲一起发展的年轻人作为骨干加以全过程培养，发挥其"传帮带"作用。通过2到3季的连续种植，青年带头人基本能够达到水稻栽培领域农艺师技术水平。其中最具代表性的恩达伊克基，原本只是布隆迪一个大学毕业后失业在家的"90后"青年。2016年，他参加了中国农业专家开展的杂交水稻种植示范项目，作为专家组培养的布隆迪第一个农民技术员。经专家组3年全方位培养，他积极发展杂交水稻，现已成长为布隆迪最年轻的政府高官和全国经济发展领导者。

三是示范带动、宣传推广，提升援外成效和水平。与援布农业示范中心有效结合，扩大示范效应。自2020年9月中国援布农业示范中心投入使用以来，中国专家组与布方工作组密切配合，杂交水稻等农业试验、农技推广工作陆续开展。专家组将占地12公顷的援布农业示范中心与各示范点工作有机结合，充分发挥各自优势开展示范推广。在示范中心建立了水稻新品种制种基地，在布全国各生态区建设示范村、推广成熟农业技术的示范培训平台，在试验（科学研究）、成果展示、人才培养等方面的作用得到充分展示。在此基础上，专家组将示范中心研究制种、平台培训与各示范村水稻品种的示范推广、实践培训紧密结合，实现充分融合对接，提升援外成效和水平。在注重宣传推广方面，布隆迪核心媒体多次对专家组的工作进行报道，如布隆迪国家电视台等当地主流媒体均对专家组的工作进行了宣传报道，让当地更多的民众了解、认知中国农业专家，让中国的先进技术遍布非洲大地。

布隆迪总统埃瓦里斯特·恩达伊施米耶为中国援布隆迪农业专家杨华德颁发功勋证书

四是创新管理，有效调动外援专家积极性。 建立完善的工作制度，保障项目顺利实施。援布隆迪高级农业专家组紧密结合农业援外专家组项目实际，制定了《农业援外专家组管理工作规范》，以制度约束专家行为，保证团队内工作生活规范有序，为推进各项工作稳步开展提供制度保障。建立团队沟通机制，加强组内信息共享。经过多年的发展和摸索，援布隆迪农业专家项目团队建立了完善的团队沟通机制。在组长的积极组织下，采取定期召开例会、聚会、个别谈心、共同参加公共活动等方式，加强组内成员沟通，把组内遇到的问题透明化，确保组内凝心聚力，共同完成援外任务。注重组内团队文化建设，提升组内团队凝聚力。援布隆迪高级农业专家组开展了一系列团队建设活动，如组内成员轮流做饭、节假日期间开展院内外散步等集体活动，有力提升了团队凝聚力。

三、成效及展望

项目实施期间，专家组借鉴中国扶贫经验，探索出"生产性投入基金"推广杂交水稻种植，选取布隆迪布班扎省基航加县林格四村作为第一个"援布水稻技术减贫示范村"进行试点，结合试验示范、技术培训、定向培养带头人等举措，帮助示范村134户1072人全体脱贫，并实现水稻生产的可持续发展。2020年，专家组在布隆迪开展了22个减贫示范村建设工作，新增受益农民超过3.1万人。布隆迪总统埃瓦里斯特·恩达伊施米耶对此高度赞赏，四次视察农业示范点，对农业组工作题词表扬，亲自授予援布隆迪农业组组长杨华德"功勋奖章"，并将利用中国水稻种植经验技术促进农业发展纳入布隆迪国家粮食安全发展规划，进一步促进布隆迪农业技术进步和产业发展、农民增收，助布加快实现"人人有所食、人人有所蓄"的目标，提升粮食安全保障水平。2022年5月10日，布隆迪环境、农业和牧业部部长鲁雷马向中国农业农村部国际交流服务中心颁发"突出贡献奖"，表彰国交中心管理实施的援布高级农业专家项目为中布农业合作作出的突出贡献。

布政府高度重视农业发展，将减贫和粮食安全战略作为政府重要发展战略，希望通过发展农业、建设农田水利设施、提升农业技术来改变这种落后的生产技术和生产方式。未来在本项目提供长期可持续的农业技术指导、进行农业技术试验示范及农业人才培训的基础上，布隆迪可进一步提升粮食种植技术及粮食产能，增强粮食安全，加快农业发展步伐。

Classic Cases of Belt and Road Agricultural Cooperation

1

South–South Cooperation Contributes to Uganda's Poverty Reduction and Development

—China-FAO-Uganda South-South Cooperation

South-South Cooperation Contributes to Uganda's Poverty Reduction and Development

—China-FAO-Uganda South-South Cooperation

Uganda is a country enjoying exceptional natural and climate conditions. Agriculture and livestock farming dominate the country's national economy, but agricultural infrastructure in the country is poor. Small family farms are prevalent. As its agricultural development is restricted by finance, technology, investment and way of farming, Uganda still faces the problem of food shortage. One of the first countries supported by the FAO-China South-South Cooperation (SSC) Program, Uganda carried out two phases of the program from 2012 to 2018. The program combines China's agricultural technology and development experience with Uganda's real conditions to spread new technology, promote new varieties and share new ideas. Beth Bechdol, Deputy Director-General at the Food and Agriculture Organization of the United Nations (FAO), said the program in Uganda was the longest and most successful country project of the China-FAO SSC Program.

I. Basic Information

Under the framework of China-FAO SSC, the Chinese government carried out two phases of the program from 2012 to 2014 and from 2016 to 2018, respectively, providing technology support in grain growing, gardening, aquatic products production and livestock breeding. The program helped Uganda improve its farming productivity and ensured food security. It also developed the country's agricultural value chain, improved the added value of agricultural products, attracted investment in agricultural sectors and increased farmers' incomes. Based on achievements made in the first phase, the second-phase program set focus on gardening, grain growing, aquatic products production, livestock breeding and agribusiness among other sectors laid out in the country's development plan for agriculture from 2016 to 2020. In implementing the two phases of program, the Chinese government sent a total of 47 agricultural experts and technicians to Uganda. They combined China's agricultural technology and development experience with Uganda's real conditions, spread new technology, promoted new varieties and shared new ideas, helping Uganda enhance food security and overall agricultural productivity. The program has achieved political, economic and social benefits. Ugandan president wrote to Chinese President Xi Jinping, applauding the achievements and expressing hopes for the launch of a new phrase. His letter received positive response from President Xi. The program in Uganda is the first SSC program both the recipient country's and the donor country's heads of state applauded in writing. It is also the first program whose third phase will be carried out with a trust fund. Thanks to the coordination by the FAO, the Ugandan government decided to contribute around $9.62 million to the FAO's unilateral trust fund to support the impending China-FAO-Uganda (third phase) SSC Program. The program is the first one under the framework of the China-FAO SSC, in which the recipient country's government made the largest contribution. It is also a fine example of giving full play to recipient country's initiative in implementing a development aid program as the China-FAO SSC trust fund successfully leveraged recipient country's funding for a development aid program.

II. Main Practices

The successful implementation of SSC in Uganda is a result of full application of a correct development approach. China's agricultural technology and development experience are combined with Uganda's real conditions. Responsibilities were well defined, a new development model was implemented, and special focus was set on capacity building.

First, participants clearly defined each other's responsibilities and obligations, and jointly made a plan for the program. FAO headquarters and its office in China both formed a management team responsible for coordinating the headquarters, regional and subregional offices. China's Ministry of Agriculture and Rural Affairs and the China Permanent Representation to FAO formed a China team for SSC project management, responsible for the implementation, coordination and following up of the program, and the making of unified standards and implementation guidelines. Uganda's Ministry of Agriculture, Animal Industry and Fisheries is responsible for implementing the SSC program. China, Uganda and the FAO jointly made the plan for the program, including its pre-planning and trilateral planning and design. The plan specified each participant's responsibilities, and collected information on projects that are being implemented in Uganda's agriculture, animal industry and fisheries and key sectors for food security to decide on participating units and organizations for the SSC program. The plan made preparations for necessary field trips and technical meetings.

Second, the Chinese expert team provided technology support to explore new approaches to agricultural development. When the planning and other preparations are made, China sent an expert team to provide technology assistance to Uganda. The Chinese experts implemented demonstration projects, promoted the application of pragmatic agricultural technology, introduced improved varieties, and carried out investigations, helping Uganda improve productivity in growing fruits, vegetables and edible mushrooms and raising fish in rice paddies. Agricultural technology involves hybrid rice, foxtail millet and pest control. While giving instructions on agricultural production, the Chinese experts helped extend the value chain with demonstration projects of processing farm produce into sweet potato powder noodles and beef jerky. They helped expand market and sales channels by connecting businesses with farmers. Introducing fish raising in rice paddies, marsh gas making, circular agriculture and leisure agriculture to Uganda, the Chinese experts also helped improve the economic, social and ecological benefits of agriculture.

Third, China provided channels so as to enhance Uganda's capacity building. Capacity building was advanced with training programs and business trips to China. training programs were launched in a variety of manners based on local conditions. They were about gardening, animal industry, hybrid rice, foxtail millet, aquatic products and marsh gas. Local people also visited China to learn about China's agricultural development, project management, application of technology, production of agriculture and animal industry, crop variety and animal breed resources, development of value chain, and corporate investment.

III. Achievements and Prospects

Through promotion of technology and China-Uganda industrial park for agricultural cooperation, China-Uganda SSC program improved Uganda's overall technology in agriculture, animal industry and fisheries, as well as the working and living quality of poor people.

First, technology and production in many areas were substantially improved. The program provided technology and know-how support in many areas, effectively enhancing Uganda's productivity in agriculture, animal industry and fisheries and ensuring the country's food security. It also helped increase farmers' incomes and fight poverty in rural areas. First, grain productivity was substantially improved. With technological assistance under the SSC framework, the yield of hybrid rice reached nine to 10 tons per hectare in Uganda, around three-folds of local high-yielding variety. The output of hybrid millet is around two to three-folds of local regular variety. With the program being implemented, 70 hectares of farmland in more than 10 administrative regions across the country were planted with millet and 60 hectares with hybrid rice. This increased farmers' incomes, realized self-reliance on grain supply, enhanced agricultural productivity, and boosted Uganda's confidence in developing agriculture and enhancing food security. Second, new gardening know-hows are of great value to large-scale agricultural production. The Chinese experts instructed Uganda's academy of agricultural sciences to breed 1.5 million plants of apple rootstock, twice as many as the total amount over the past four years. The experts tested growing edible mushrooms and potatoes, and carried out experiments on controlling mango fruit flies and citrus black spot. The expertise is of great value to large-scale agricultural production. Third, the Chinese experts developed the animal industry. They used ammoniated forage and planted elephant grass to solve the problem with forage quality and shortage in dry season, increasing the nutrients of stalks and making them more edible for livestock. To lower the cost of coops and make them affordable to chicken farmers, the Chinese experts designed wooden coops and promoted them among farmers, making it possible to scale up the chicken farm and raise chicken in an intensive manner. Fourth, the Chinese experts invented new ways of raising aquatic products. They launched six demonstration projects of fishing ground design, fry hatching, fry transportation, aquafarm design, fishing raising in rice paddies, and fodder processing. The daily output of a small-scale fodder processing practice reached 800kg. Fry hatching rate was enhanced from 20% to 80%. The survival rate of fry after transportation grew from 79% to more than 98%. Raising fish in rice paddies has become a new way of increasing incomes for local farmers.

Chinese expert reaps a bumper harvest of hybrid rice.

Second, the construction of the China-Uganda industrial park for agricultural cooperation improved the quality of the working and living quality. The program combined development cooperation with investment promotion. While providing practical agricultural technology for Uganda's agricultural development, it brought in the private sector to build the China-Uganda industrial park for agricultural cooperation. This greatly improved local infrastructure, extended the value chain of agricultural production, and enhanced the quality of farmers' the working and living quality of farmers. First, the Chinese experts solved problems regarding technology, agricultural means of production and market. The industrial park adopted a "business + smallholder" approach, providing local farmers with improved crop variety, agricultural means of production and free technology services. It purchased agricultural products per contract and built a bridge to connect farmers with the market. So far, the industrial park has provided necessary supplies and technology guidance to farmers in 840 hectares of rice growing region. The core industrial park led other places in boosting agricultural development. Second, the program improved the infrastructure in rural areas, providing guarantee for agricultural production and people's livelihoods. The industrial park invested $200,000 in digging three wells and building four pools, providing farming and drinking water for more than 1,200 farmers in the neighboring area. This move was warmly applauded by local people. Third, the industrial park created more jobs and channels for farmers to increase their incomes. The management of the industrial park has six members recruited from local people with an undergraduate degree or above certified by European and American universities. A total of 216 permanent jobs on engineering and field management have been created in the demonstration region, and some 1,000 casual workers were recruited for seasonal farming work. Local people take pride in working in the industrial park. As the construction of the industrial park is advanced, it is expected to boost direct employment of around 10,000 people.

Since 2009, China, Uganda and the FAO have been conducting SSC to remove primary obstacles for crop growing, fisheries, animal industry, the development of other key agricultural sectors and the processing of agricultural products. The first two phases of the program made remarkable achievements. To improve Uganda's overall agricultural productivity, the three sides initiated the third phase of the program in 2023. Efforts will be centered on building a base for technology transfer, making plans for increasing rice and millet outputs, supporting the upgrading of the animal industry, and developing the value chain of aquaculture. The aim is to consolidate achievements made in the first two phases, apply suitable Chinese technology on a larger scale, and help Uganda transform its agriculture. While feeding its population, the country's agricultural industry is expected to become commercial and generate earnings.

2

Working Together for A Platform of Global Division of Labor and Cooperation

—China-Indonesia "Two Countries, Twin Parks" Project

Working Together for A Platform of Global Division of Labor and Cooperation
—China-Indonesia "Two Countries, Twin Parks" Project

Fujian Province as a core area of the 21st Century Maritime Silk Road has close economic and trade relations with ASEAN and Indonesia is a major hub where overseas Chinese from Fujian have gathered. The two sides have shared a time-honored history of exchanges. The idea of "two countries, twin parks" for China and Indonesia (hereinafter referred to as China-Indonesia "Two Countries, Twin Parks") was proposed in 2018 by Fuqing City, a famous hometown of overseas Chinese, to explore a twin-park cooperation mechanism with the interconnectivity of industries, interoperability between infrastructure, and reciprocity in policy. With China's Yuanhong Investment Zone and Indonesia's Bintan Industrial Park, Aviarna Industrial Park and Batang Industrial Park as mainstays, a platform of global division of labor and cooperation, dedicated to developing industrial and supply chains, is created as a green channel for investment and trade between the two sides, making China-Indonesia "Two Countries, Twin Parks" a major platform undertaking related cooperation projects under the Belt and Road Initiative.

I. Basic Information

The idea of "two countries, twin parks" represents a new model of industrial capacity cooperation in which two sovereign countries build industrial parks in each other's territories for joint development. In light of their development strategies and bilateral economic and trade collaboration, China and Indonesia aim to build demonstration parks for economic and trade innovation and growth as grounding the efforts in the new development stage, applying the new development philosophy, fostering a new development paradigm, and deepening cross-border cooperation towards ASEAN. The project pursues a solid, efficient and innovative model of global division of labor and cooperation through industrial, supply and value chains and paves a strategic corridor for a double development paradigm withdomestic circulation being the mainstay and the two circulations reinforcing each other to foster pilot demonstration parks that launch a new round of opening up and cooperation. Internationalized high-end industrial parks which embrace "specialization, innovation, greenness and openness" are built as key hubs for the distribution of bulk food, ingredients, fruits and meat and important channels for the double development paradigm. Through cooperation, the economic, trade and cultural exchanges between China and Indonesia are intensified comprehensively, and upon the advantage of overseas Chinese from Fujian who are all over the world, a brand for the hometown of overseas Chinese is shaped to represent their culture and nostalgia, through which the demonstration parks for economic and trade innovation and growth will become popular for new and old overseas Chinese returning to start businesses and be built into a new window for overseas Chinese to communicate closely, a new platform for service trade and investment cooperation, and a new center for economic and high-end industrial cooperation between China and Indonesia.

Currently, the Chinese industrial park has extended its industrial chains of key sectors including marine economy, food processing and cross-border trade and sped up the cooperation in marine fisheries, equipment manufacturing, halal food, cold-chain logistics, green mining, light industry and textile industry so as to foster a "global center of fisheries" and a new driver for the growth of marine economy together with Indonesia.

II. Main Practices

The China-Indonesia "Two Countries, Twin Parks", an exploration of the twin-park cooperation mechanism with the interconnectivity of industries, interoperability between infrastructure, and reciprocity in policy, which adopts a new model of industrial capacity cooperation in which China and Indonesia build industrial parks in each other's territories for joint development, is of great significance in utilizing complementary advantages, revitalizing superior resources, improving relevant industrial and supply chains, and facilitating economic and trade exchanges between the two countries.

First, the working mechanism is improved. There have established the Joint Working Committee on China-Indonesia "Two Countries, Twin Parks" and vice-ministerial (provincial) consultations as well as a mechanism for multilevel action among the Ministry of Commerce of the People's Republic of China, Fujian Province, Fuzhou City and Fuqing City to coordinate the park construction. On the provincial level, Fujian Province organized a leading group for the construction of "twin parks", headed by the executive vice governor and the vice governor in charge, and a task force to apply a weekly meeting system. On the city level, Fuzhou City set up a leading group and an economic and trade matchmaking group for the integration of resources and forces across the board and the efficient coordination and implementation of multifarious tasks. Fuqing City innovated the development and operation pattern of "Command+ Management Committee+ Investors+ Industry Fund+ Think Tank" and founded the "Two Countries, Twin Parks" Holding Group so as to advance the high-level, standardized construction in an all-round way.

Second, a dialogue mechanism is established. The Ministry of Commerce of the People's Republic of China and the People's Government of Fujian Province have been working for a smooth dialogue mechanism with Indonesian authorities since 2021. On March 23, 2021, the first session of the Joint Working Committee on China-Indonesia "Two Countries, Twin Parks" was co-chaired by Zhang Xiangchen, former Vice Minister of Commerce of the People's Republic of China, together with Guo Ningning, Vice Governor of Fujian Province, and Ayodhia Kalake, Indonesia's Deputy Coordinating Minister of Marine and Investment Affairs, via videolink and announced the official launch of the Joint Working Committee on China-Indonesia "Two Countries, Twin Parks". On June 16, 2023, a consultation among the Department of Asian Affairs, Ministry of Commerce of the People's Republic of China, and the Economic and Commercial Office of the Embassy of the People's Republic of China in the Republic of Indonesia, Fujian Province's Department of Commerce and Foreign Affairs Office, Fuzhou City and Fuzhou Customs, and Indonesian Coordinating Ministry of Marine and Investment Affairs was held to push forward the construction of "twin parks", and five consensuses were reached. On August 31, 2023, the second session of the Joint Working Committee on China-Indonesia "Two Countries, Twin Parks" was held in Fuzhou City, where representatives of the People's Government of Fuzhou City and Indonesian industrial parks respectively put forward the matters that need mutual promotion, and conducted in-depth and detailed exchanges over the joint working mechanism of park managers, the preparation of park development schemes, the progress of trade and investment facilitation, and supporting policies, and reached an agreement on the next step of cooperation for the construction of "twin parks".

Third, policy enablement is enhanced. To further concentrate resources to the parks, making the Chinese industrial park into a blessed zone enabled by policies, openness and investment towards high-quality development, Fujian Province's Department of Commerce has taken the lead in formulating a number of special policy initiatives on the provincial level, while seeking out certain policies and measures from national ministries and commissions, mainly involving the guarantee of factors as well as industries, finance and taxation, customs clearance and human resources, which are currently in progress of declaring, approving, and finalizing the issuance and implementation. In addition, Fujian Province will soon promulgate and implement the *Implementation Scheme for the Construction of China-Indonesia Economic and Trade Innovation and Growth Demonstration Parks* and the *Fujian Provincial Special Policies and Measures for the Construction of China-Indonesia Economic and Trade Innovation and Growth Demonstration Parks*.

Aerial view of the Chinese industrial park
—Yuanhong Investment Zone in Fuzhou City

III. Achievements and Prospects

First, the scale of investment between China and Indonesia has continued to grow. A number of major projects have been kicked off and put into operation since the approval of China-Indonesia "Two Countries, Twin Parks", which have strongly empowered the industrial bearing capacity of both sides. The construction of China-Indonesia "Two Countries, Twin Parks" has been on a fast track since 2023. In February 2023, the Indonesia-Fuzhou Economic and Trade Matchmaking Meeting and Project Signing Ceremony was held in Jakarta, Indonesia, and 15 projects were signed in a centralized manner, with a total investment of RMB21.6 billion. In May, the China (Fujian)-Indonesia "Two Countries, Twin Parks" Joint Construction and Economic and Trade Cooperation Promotion was held in Jakarta, Indonesia, where 21 projects were signed on site, with a total amount of up to RMB43.2 billion. At the China (Fujian)-ASEAN Economic and Trade Cooperation Forum held in Fuzhou City on August 6, another nine projects were signed to involve a total investment of nearly RMB30 billion. As of August 2023, the Chinese industrial park has attracted 620 commercial enterprises and 66 investment projects with a gross investment of RMB90.551 billion, when 17 projects have been invested by Chinese enterprises in Indonesia, amounting to RMB39.93 billion.

Second, the bilateral economic and trade relations have reached new heights. Fueled by the "Two Countries, Twin Parks" project, the economic and trade cooperation between China (mainly Fujian) and Indonesia has grown rapidly. In 2022, Indonesia became Fujian's top trading partner in ASEAN as the volume of imports and exports amounted to RMB121.52 billion, rising by 32.2% compared with a year earlier. China has maintained the status as Indonesia's largest trading partner for eight consecutive years and continues to be its third largest source of investment. Indonesia's *Jakarta Post* wrote that over the past 20 years, China has been Indonesia's most important partner, especially in economic development, investment and trade. Underpinned by China's Belt and Road Initiative and Indonesia's "Global Maritime Axis" concept, the two sides will step up cooperation in infrastructure sectors.

Third, bilateral exchanges and cooperation become increasingly closer. The China-Indonesia "Two Countries, Twin Parks" project facilitates maritime interconnectivity, investment and trade, cultural exchanges and cooperation between the two sides. The cooperation concentrates on marine fisheries, mining, infrastructure, culture and tourism and taps the potential of working on clean energy, new materials and textiles. Now several Indonesian research centers have been set up in Fujian Province; the Indonesian language major has been offered in universities; and the number of Indonesian students studying in China is growing day by day. Educational cooperation has sown the seeds for the two sides to establish friendly ties and achieve better understanding.

In view of the later developments, China-Indonesia "Two Countries, Twin Parks" will continue to advocate the Silk Road Spirit—peace and cooperation, openness and inclusiveness, mutual learning and mutual benefit—and follow the principle of extensive consultation, joint contribution and shared benefits in reinforcing the development fruits, so as to make the twin parks mutually beneficial from the cooperation.

First, greater breakthroughs in policy will be pursued. Policies and measures favoring the construction of Indonesian industrial parks, in terms of investment and trade access, registration and declaration, cross-border identification of human resources, offshore fishing, aquaculture, customs clearance facilitation, tax incentives, etc., will be rolled out to bring more Chinese enterprises into Indonesian industrial parks.

Second, leading companies will be grown bigger and stronger to boost industrial clusters. To begin with marine fisheries, China and Indonesia will work together to foster industrial and supply chains around five major industries: marine fisheries, tropical agriculture, light and textile industries, machinery and electronics, and green mining. Leading companies will be grown bigger and stronger to attract investments and extend, replace or reinforce the chains. Their entrance will bring in upstream and downstream businesses to boost the scale of two-way trade and industrial clusters within the park.

Third, new progress will be made in subject matters. As to facilitate the communication, collaboration and mutual support of the Customs of both countries, it needs to establish an industrial cooperation promotion center and a joint customs group for China-Indonesia "Two Countries, Twin Parks" as well as a China-Indonesia Customs coordination mechanism.

3

"Sweet" Cooperation under the Belt and Road Initiative

—Ethiopian Sugar Factory Project

"Sweet" Cooperation under the Belt and Road Initiative

—Ethiopian Sugar Factory Project

China and Ethiopia are both ancient civilizations and have shared a time-honored history of friendly ties. Their relations have been a good example of China-Africa cooperation. In particular, the two have worked together even more extensively following the launch of the Belt and Road Initiative. Since 2013, China CAMC Engineering Corporation Limited (hereinafter referred to as CAMCE), affiliated to China National Machinery Industry Corporation, has fulfilled the Belt and Road Initiative with intensified sugar cooperation with Ethiopia, and yielded impressive social benefits. It set a good example of China-Africa cooperation and demonstrated a good international image of China.

I. Basic Information

Ethiopian coffee is world-famous and Ethiopians love coffee. Sugar is a daily necessity for Ethiopians. However, the gap in sugar supply remains quite large due to insufficient sugar productivity in Ethiopia. Ethiopia has a population of over 100 million. Its annual demand for sugar is approximately 1.4 million tons, calculated by the African average consumption of 14kg of sugar per person per year, but its annual sugar output is less than 300,000 tons, registering a gap of over 1.1 million tons. Despite the fact that local climate and land conditions are favorable for sugarcane planting, every year, Ethiopia spends hundreds of millions of dollars in foreign exchange importing sugar for its low sugar productivity and absence of processing techniques. Accordingly, there are imminent strategic needs for Ethiopia to improve its sugar productivity and processing techniques. In 2009, the construction of sugar plants was kicked off one after another and a large amount of land expropriated from farmers for sugarcane planting in Ethiopia. Unfortunately, the construction was halted due to construction and management deficiencies, delays and serious cost overruns.

Being an active practitioner of the Belt and Road Initiative, CAMCE develops three business sectors—design consulting and engineering contracting; development and application of advanced engineering techniques and equipment; and engineering investment and operation—and offers integrated services such as survey and design, planning consultation, financing and investment, procurement and supply of complete sets of equipment, construction and project management, and operation and maintenance, etc. Learning about Ethiopia's sugar development program, CAMCE took the initiative and came up with elaborate plans when it decided to help Ethiopia boost the sugar industry. With professional advantages, it contracted the construction of Welkait Sugar Factory with a processing capacity of 24,000 TCD located in northern Ethiopia for the first time in 2013, which was highly received and praised by the Ethiopian government and society for the efficient progress and excellent strength. In this context, CAMCE continued to finish the construction of Tana Beles No.1 Sugar Factory project entrusted by Ethiopia Sugar Corporation (ESC) in 2019. The completion took two years of hard work and overcame the COVID-19 pandemic, the Ethiopian civil war, material shortages, and many other difficulties. The Tana Beles No.1 Sugar Factory was put into operation and produced sugar on June 6, 2021. In May 2022, at the invitation of the owner ESC, CAMCE successfully signed the operation contract for the project. In April 2023 when finishing the tests on completion and performance, it was again entrusted by the owner and signed the operation contract for the project in 2023.

II. Main Practices

Since the launch of the project, CAMCE has participated in its construction throughout the organization of the project management team, business contract management, subcontractor bidding, project implementation, HR training, cost control, quality and safety management, and brand building.

First, the project has been planned and laid out in an all-inclusive fashion and applied process management. At the early stage of development and design, CAMCE conducted on-site inspections, data collection and in-depth analysis of the project design, equipment and construction conditions, and completed the supplementary design and equipment selection and determined a sound program for construction quickly and professionally. The project adopted the conceptual design of India and the equipment came from Germany, China, India, etc. In the implementation, each team thoroughly took in original technical ideas and the equipment features and considered actual conditions and operations afterwards when organizing personnel for refined construction, successfully completing the continued construction of each system. The in-depth and efficient communication with local governments and owners was promoted actively, and the standardized operations and strict technical control were highly praised by supervisors and owners. With experience of production and operations in Chinese sugar factories, technicians of the project department came up with more than 1,000 suggestions and measures for the improvement of old techniques and equipment in light of Ethiopian conditions to make them more efficient.

Aerial view of Tana Beles No.1 Sugar Factory in Ethiopia

Second, it has been deeply rooted in the sustainable development strategy for green construction. CAMCE adheres to scientific construction that prioritizes environmental protection and efficiency and upholds sustainable development in practice. As to build an environmentally friendly project with excellence, its philosophy of "green design, green engineering, green manufacturing and green industry" was integrated into the implementation. The project includes a sewage treatment station with a daily treatment capacity of 6,000 cubic meters. The project department of CAMCE has tested BOD, COD5, dissolved oxygen and other indicators of drainage on a regular basis to ensure that the discharged wastewater meets the standard for irrigation water. The treated wastewater could be used to irrigate sugarcane fields directly, so this has protected the local ecological environment and saved water resources. CAMCE also formulated a number of construction-related management measures for environmental protection, covering the disposal of waste soil, transportation of construction waste and installation-consumable waste, dust control at the site, discharge of waste gas and wastewater, etc., and equipped with a full-time safety management team for supervision, which was normalized to make sure that environmental protection measures are well implemented.

Third, it has promoted extensive consultation, joint contribution and shared benefits and supported local coordinated development. Ethiopia's industrial development is backward relatively, and most of the specialized equipment in sugar factories depends on imports. The project department of CAMCE, following the principle of extensive consultation, joint contribution and shared benefits, has combined China's advanced construction techniques with the Ethiopian project according to local conditions, which not only met the requirement specification but provided quality engineering services for the smooth progress of the project within the time limit. A large number of local constructors in civil engineering, electrical installation, structure installation, and insulation engineering were chosen for the project, contributing to the growth of local companies. Among them, "ABIYU ILLU CONTRACTOR" was a representative of excellent local subcontractors. CAMCE also pursued localized management and operations when recruiting management personnel and construction units. It has worked hard to create jobs for local population, and at the peak of construction, over 800 of the construction crew with 1,000 workers at the site were from local places.

Ethiopian teenagers holding sugar in their hands

III. Achievements and Prospects

First, it reduces the sugar shortage and saves a lot of foreign exchange for Ethiopia. The Tana Beles No.1 Sugar Factory, when operating at full capacity, can daily process 12,000 tons of sugarcane to produce 1,500 tons of refined sugar per day and 200,000 tons of white sugar annually, thereby saving USD120 million in foreign exchange every year. These foreign exchanges are used to import edible oil, wheat and other urgently needed food crops and products, creating favorable conditions for the entire country to develop sustainably.

Second, it broadens the access to employment and contributes to HR training. The Tana Beles No.1 Sugar Factory has created a large number of employment opportunities for local people. During the period of operation, it offers jobs for 5,000 sugarcane planters, 4,000 sugarcane harvesters and 1,000 skilled workers for the factory running. The construction and operation periods have stimulated the growth of upstream and downstream companies of building materials and construction consumables and made local community economy, housing, catering, animal husbandry, community healthcare and education and other sectors thrive rapidly. What's more, Chinese team composed of over 20 engineers and more than 70 operators passed on advanced sugar-producing techniques and thermal-power-station operations to local engineers and workers through the uninterrupted duty between two shifts in the period of operations, which has trained lots of sugar-producing technicians and skilled workers to improve the management and technology in Ethiopia.

Third, it achieves a balance between green, low-carbon growth and economic benefits. The Tana Beles No.1 Sugar Factory uses boilers to burn sugarcane bagasse to generate the electricity and steam needed for the production equipment, and the generated carbon dioxide is absorbed by growing sugarcane. The by-product molasses can be used to make feed and alcohol and the silt and slag as fertilizer for sugarcane after processing. The Tana Beles No.1 Sugar Factory is a real green factory. Its two 25MW generator sets can transmit 240MWH of electricity to the outside per day as satisfying the consumption of production, alleviating the pressure on local power grid and creating additional economic benefits of USD600,000 or so every year.

Fourth, it creates and delivers the value of China's excellent projects.

The Tana Beles No.1 Sugar Factory project actively serves the national diplomacy and responds to the Belt and Road Initiative. It has been widely concerned and covered multiple times by mainstream media in China and abroad, including ETV, People's Daily, Xinhuanet, and China Media Group, and has been unanimously received by all walks of life in Ethiopia. The Prime Minister of Ethiopia, Abiy Ahmed Ali, said that the project bears the hope of the Ethiopian people and is a "concrete livelihood project". The governments of states and cities have taken the sugar factory as an educational base for students of different school ages.

The successful performance testing, production and operations of the Tana Beles No.1 Sugar Factory is a milestone in the history of Ethiopian sugar development and a turning point of CAMCE integrating investment, construction and operation in the African market.

Going forward, CAMCE will continue to uphold the principle of extensive consultation, joint contribution and shared benefits in deepening the strategic cooperation on sugar production with Ethiopia and other countries in Africa and push forward local economic and social advancement. It will actively fulfill social responsibilities, support global poverty reduction with vigorous efforts, and strive to turn each project into a bond connecting the peoples of the two countries and a bridge for deepening their friendship, so as to advance the Belt and Road Initiative with high-level contributions and work for a community with a shared future for mankind with its strength and wisdom.

4

Advancement of Brunei-Guangxi Economic Corridor (BGEC)

—Hiseaton Fisheries (B) Sdn Bhd Project

Advancement of Brunei-Guangxi Economic Corridor (BGEC)

—Hiseaton Fisheries (B) Sdn Bhd Project

Brunei is one of the ASEAN countries with good diplomatic relations and frequent exchanges and cooperation with China. Since the Belt and Road Initiative was launched, the economic and trade cooperation between China and Brunei has grown rapidly, and the Brunei-Guangxi Economic Corridor has been steadily advancing as one of the two flagship projects. The Brunei-China (Guangxi) Fisheries Cooperation Demonstration Zone project undertaken by Guangxi Hiseaton Food Co., Ltd. (Guangxi Hiseaton), the first project in progress under the Brunei-Guangxi Economic Corridor, has been implemented successfully and achieved remarkable outcomes, thanks to national support and the vigorous effort of Guangxi Zhuang Autonomous Region.

I. Basic Information

Guangxi Hiseaton cultivates, processes, and sells marine aquatic products in China and overseas. It began to develop offshore large cages for the R&D and aquaculture of marine fishes in 2009 and was also the first company in Guangxi that developed large-scale mariculture. In recent years, to avoid natural disasters and typhoons and seek better development, the company has responded to the Belt and Road Initiative actively and "gone global" to look for suitable places for mariculture growth. After repeated inspections in many ASEAN countries since 2012, it was finally confirmed that Brunei is the best place for deep-sea cage culture. Brunei has a tropical rainforest climate. Its seawater temperature is constant at 28℃ all year round; hydrological conditions are good; and the waters are pollution-free and typhoon-free, making it so perfect for cage culture. However, there was a strong realistic demand for attracting investment and stimulating industrial development in Brunei since local aquaculture technology remained backward, fishery technicians were lacking, and many technical problems in offshore aquaculture needed to be solved urgently.

The People's Government of Guangxi Zhuang Autonomous Region, Government of Brunei and Guangxi Hiseaton have promoted bilateral cooperation actively in light of China's national policies, Brunei's needs, and corporate aspirations. With multiple exchanges and negotiations, Guangxi Hiseaton reached a consensus with Brunei and signed a Framework Agreement for Cooperation with Bruneian authorities in June 2016. By the Framework Agreement for Cooperation, Guangxi Hiseaton invested RMB10 million for the founding of Hiseaton Fisheries (B) Sdn Bhd in Brunei that develops fry breeding, culture, purchase, processing and sales of marine aquatic products. The Government of Brunei approved of granting Hiseaton Fisheries (B) Sdn Bhd the right to use 2,000 hectares of offshore waters, 22 hectares of hatcheries, and two hectares of product processing sites, and furthermore, the Brunei Fisheries Development Center was offered for use at a lower rent.

With a gross investment of RMB130 million, the Brunei-China

(Guangxi) Fishery Cooperation Demonstration Zone project consists of a center and four functional areas—Joint Research Center on Aquatic Science and Technology, Deep-sea Aquaculture Cage Base, Feed and Product Processing Base, Fry Breeding Base, and Warehousing and Logistics Base, covering an area of up to 20.2 square kilometers, and is to be implemented in two five-year plans. Up to now, the first phase of construction, including the Fry Breeding Base and Deep-sea Aquaculture Cage Base, has been completed to ensure the conservation and selection of cultured species.

II. Main Practices

Brunei is rich in fishery resources but subjected to a weak foundation for fisheries, insufficient industrial supporting facilities and industrial and supply chains, and a lack of aquaculture technology. Hiseaton Fisheries (B) Sdn Bhd has invested in infrastructure construction under the authorization of the Government of Brunei and recruited teams for R&D and breeding. Meanwhile, relying on Guangxi Hiseaton's years of aquaculture technology and its cooperation mechanism with the Chinese Academy of Fishery Sciences (CAFS) to offer technical support for the Brunei-China (Guangxi) Fishery Cooperation Demonstration Zone project, aquaculture technology has been localized and technical training widely carried out. Hiseaton Fisheries (B) Sdn Bhd has contributed Bruneian research achievements and experience to China's fisheries while bringing China's advanced technology to benefit Brunei's fisheries. It is the way they share development outcomes and learn from each other's development experience.

First, infrastructure construction is launched as fundamental support for industrial development. To develop fishery culture in Brunei, breeding and aquaculture bases must be first built on account of the weak foundation and insufficiency of infrastructure there. The Brunei-China (Guangxi) Fishery Cooperation Demonstration Zone project is mainly composed of a fry breeding base, a deep-sea aquaculture cage base, and an international R&D exchange and training center, in which the former two constitute the Core Industrial Area and the latter serves as the R&D Demonstration Area. The Core Industrial Area is divided for parent culture, food-organism culture, fry culture, large-scale fry culture, commercial aquaculture, and product processing. The parent culture area provides fertilized eggs for hatching; the food-organism culture area provides feed; the fry culture area and large-scale fry culture area cultivate hatched larvae and large-scale fry respectively; the commercial aquaculture area cultivates commercial fish; and the product processing area finishes the "fishing—transportation—pre-processing—freezing—refrigeration—detection—delivery" process from the deep-sea aquaculture cage base. With the support of the above-mentioned infrastructure construction, a full industrial chain through "fish seed—fry breeding—culture—feed—processing" has been formed in Brunei's aquatic zones by Hiseaton Fisheries (B) Sdn Bhd.

Second, technology transfer is realized relying on the technology accumulation in China. To take root in Brunei, technology plays a decisive role in addition to completing the above-mentioned infrastructure construction. Technical support is indispensable from ensuring the survival rate of imported fry at the early stage to subsequent culture and breeding. However, it is impossible to have Chinese technology completely applied to Brunei, since the country lacks corresponding technology and its climate and hydrological conditions are different from China. To address this problem, Hiseaton Fisheries (B) Sdn Bhd, with the resources of parent company in China, has established long-term and close cooperation with CAFS and other specialized organizations over the years and invited experts to Brunei multiple times for guidance and training based on local conditions. Continuous technical adjustments have enabled the localization of fry supply for the first time, providing strong support for the sustainable development of local fisheries.

Large deep-sea commercial aquaculture base

Third, cooperation and exchanges are developed extensively for the training of local fishery talent. The long-term growth of fisheries is inseparable from fishery talent. Hiseaton Fisheries (B) Sdn Bhd took the lead and initiated a China-Brunei fishery S&T cooperation platform together with Bruneian research institutes (Universiti Brunei Darussalam (UBD), Brunei Fisheries Development Center, and IBTE) and Chinese research institutes (Shanghai Ocean University, and CAFC). It currently has reached intentions of cooperation with Universiti Teknologi Brunei (UTB), UBD and Brunei Vocational and Technical College. Teaching and internship bases have been arranged in the research center and culture bases and technicians are hired as part-time lecturers to offer charitable training and education of aquatic talent in Brunei. What's more, the Demonstration Zone has formed stable and in-depth ties with China's research institutes such as Guangxi Academy of Fishery Sciences, and South China Sea Fisheries Research Institute, Chinese Academy of Fishery Sciences (SCSFRI, CAFS) to bring in outstanding Chinese talent for joint research and technology transfer so as to improve the platform's R&D strength and influence in Southeast Asia. Hiseaton Fisheries (B) Sdn Bhd has offered vocational and technical training for local and migrant fishermen from the Brunei Darussalam-Indonesia-Malaysia-Philippines East ASEAN Growth Area (BIMP-EAGA) since 2016 as a solution to the shortage of local fishery technicians. Over the years, the training has produced good brand effect. Now a consensus is reached among Hiseaton Fisheries (B) Sdn Bhd, Brunei Aquaculture Development Center, Sanya Tropical Fisheries Research Institute, and UBD on improving the training in level and scope.

III. Achievements and Prospects

Supported by the governments and agricultural authorities of China and Brunei, the construction of the Demonstration Zone is progressing smoothly, and brilliant results have been achieved in Brunei aquaculture. The project implementation has contributed greatly to the advancement of Brunei's fisheries, China's diplomatic cause, and the Belt and Road Initiative. As to boost local fisheries, the entrance of Hiseaton Fisheries (B) Sdn Bhd created three "firsts" in Brunei as follows.

One is the localization of fry supply which is realized for the first time. This ended the history that Brunei relied on the import of fry for aquaculture and successfully launched comprehensive captive breeding of tropical fish for profit. **Another is the establishment of the first offshore marine pasture.** In the relevant waters off Brunei, 24 large cages and 178 small cages were installed and put into use, a breakthrough in the history of zero marine pasture of Brunei. **The last is the first export of marine cultured fish to Canada, the United States and other countries.**

As an important export-oriented industry in China, fisheries play a pioneering role in the agricultural cooperation with foreign countries. In recent years, Guangxi Hiseaton has grown rapidly with deepened cooperation with the outside world. As a good example of "going global", the company has been actively engaged in public service activities such as local talent training while spurring the growth of local industries. It is also a practitioner of mutually beneficial cooperation and a successful case that reinforces cooperation and exchanges with BRI neighboring countries and boosts the confidence of business entities in sovereign countries to work together for shared benefits.

In the future, the Demonstration Zone is ready to foster an industrial chain that focuses on industrial development and "integrates" species selection, fry breeding, culture, feed production, processing and sales, with pilot deep-sea cage culture and research support and based upon species selection and breeding, so as to drive the growth of manufacturing, fishery services, trade and transportation. It will first work to improve its operational capabilities by refining supporting facilities and completing the installation and operation of facilities and equipment in processing and ice plants. Besides, it will develop organizations and mechanisms to make the administration more internationalized and specialized. Next, as to improve technological innovation capabilities, an expert consultation system and a talent introduction and training system will be launched. Furthermore, service systems for policy consultation, investment analysis, fund raising, production service, risk control, marketing, technical standards, quality and safety, and information and liaison are to be established to enhance industrial agglomeration and international competitiveness.

5

Boosting Rural Revitalization of Laos with China's Experience

— "Asia-Potash" Working for Rural Development of Laos

Boosting Rural Revitalization of Laos with China's Experience

—"Asia-Potash" Working for Rural Development of Laos

Asia-Potash International Investment (Guangzhou) Co., Ltd. (hereinafter referred to as "Asia-Potash") is an international company specializing in potash mining and potash fertilizer production and sales. Having been dedicated to Lao potash industry for 14 years, it has become a Chinese-funded model in Laos. As producing potash fertilizer in Laos, Asia-Potash has paid close attention to the agricultural and rural development there. It has developed modern agriculture and industries for poverty alleviation through tapping the potential of agricultural resources in Laos and devoted to local services. These have contributed to the rural development of Laos, showcased a vibrant, harmonious and responsible image of Chinese companies, and laid a solid foundation for the cooperation between China and Laos.

I. Basic Information

Asia-Potash is the first potash company in Laos to realize industrialized mining. It launched a one-million-ton potash project in 2020, and only took 17 months to complete the construction and commissioning and reach the production capacity and standards as required, known as "Asia-Potash Speed". On December 31, 2022, its second one-million-ton potash fertilizer project was also completed, and Asia-Potash became the largest potash fertilizer producer in Southeast Asia. Currently, its third million-ton potash project has been kicked off and is expected to achieve a production capacity of three million tons by the end of 2023 and a production capacity of five million tons of potash fertilizer in 2025. By then, Asia-Potash will become a global top supplier of potash fertilizer. Its potash fertilizer has also been supplied to China and is an important source of domestic imports in addition to supplying Southeast Asian countries.

Laos is the only landlocked country in Southeast Asia, where agriculture depends entirely on the weather, with weak irrigation facilities, frequent plant diseases and insect pests, and backward technology. Even today, as Lao agriculture is still stuck in the extensive cultivation of peasant economy with low efficiency, the income and living standards of farmers remain at a low level and the incidence of poverty in rural areas is about 30%. Agricultural development and rural poverty reduction have been the pursuit of the Government of Lao PDR for many years. Deeply rooted in Laos over these years, Asia-Potash has paid great attention to its rural development and poverty reduction while working for its development. Drawing on China's practices and experience in alleviating poverty, it has promoted modern agriculture, launched poverty alleviation projects by developing industries, built a platform of agricultural technology training, and invested in local infrastructure construction in Laos, which achieved good outcomes and were highly received and praised by Laos.

II. Main Practices

First, modern agriculture is advanced with the introduction of new varieties, technologies and models. Agriculture is a pillar of economy in Laos. Rice and vegetables are the most important crops and the area of rice cultivation accounts for 85% of crop growing area nationwide. When over 70% of residents across the country only grow rice for one season, the backwardness of agricultural technology results in low rice yield, only about 200-300 kilograms per mu, so the basic needs of many farmers have not been satisfied yet. Fortunately, Laos has perfect natural conditions for agriculture thanks to rich resources and abundant precipitation and heat. In view of this situation, Asia-Potash introduced China's rice cultivation technology and hybrid varieties of rice, and developed 110 hectares of three-season rice cultivation in Khong District of Champasak province for demonstration, with a 1,200-hectare water conservancy project as the support. Centralized production and management of large-scale rice are adopted; and excellent varieties of rice, quality and high-yield multi-season rice cultivation technology, and modern agriculture equipment were imported to Laos in cooperation with China's rice cultivation teams. The efficiency of production has been improved largely as Asia-Potash purchased large automated combine harvesters and used large drones for sowing, fertilizing and spraying pesticides, etc. The company has also formed an "ecological + industrial" development model. It is, by relying on the advantage of ecological resources and following the "rice-fishery ecology plus circular cultivation and breeding" model, experimenting multi-season rice cultivation and shaping a system of "rice and fishery symbiosis", through which a standardized and comprehensive demonstration base for rice cultivation and fishery breeding comes into being to fulfill the ecological development goal of "one field, double harvests". The company also presented potash fertilizer to farmers and promoted scientific techniques of fertilization to raise the production and income of villagers.

Inauguration Ceremony of Asia-Potash Three-Season Rice Cultivation for Modern Agriculture

Second, poverty alleviation projects by developing industries are launched to lift local villagers out of poverty. Land transfer and large-scale cultivation are advocated. Asia-Potash has guided farmers in a poverty-stricken village of Khammouane province to voluntarily transfer land to form contiguous areas for unified cultivation towards intensive, large-scale and modern management of land, so as to improve the efficiency of land use and the income of farmers. Vegetable greenhouses are developed. Based on local climate conditions, Asia-Potash built 45 vegetable greenhouses with an investment of RMB560,000 in the village and introduced a number of new, exotic and special varieties of vegetables from abroad to develop distinctive crops for profit. A demonstration farm of livestock and poultry husbandry is built. As to support local animal husbandry, Asia-Potash has brought in Yunnan Xishuangbanna Livestock & Poultry Technology Co., Ltd. and built a livestock and poultry husbandry farm mainly for broilers, with an annual output of 144,000 broilers. All the vegetables and livestock and poultry produce of farmers are purchased by the company and sold to the canteens in mining areas.

Third, a technology training platform is bridged to cultivate technical talent for local agriculture. "If you give a man a fish, you feed him for a day. If you teach a man to fish, you feed him for a lifetime." Asia-Potash has taken many measures to build the platform for agricultural technology cooperation, demonstration and promotion, and talent training and cultivate technical talent for Laos through training. It has strived to improve the production skills of local villagers and lift them out of poverty to become rich. The modern agriculture project team of Asia-Potash has successively sent agricultural technicians to Laos for field research and scientific analysis. Relying on the experimental bases of multi-season rice and vegetables for modern agriculture, it carried out the research and demonstration on the graded flood irrigation technology by seedling stages for multi-season rice and taught Lao farmers to grow rice and vegetables step by step. In addition, the company held nine training sessions on vegetable cultivation technology in the village, and many villagers learned the way to do it. Among them, 18 farmers started small vegetable gardening in front of and behind their houses, and gained increased income.

Fourth, employment channels are broadened and job opportunities increased for villagers. For the villagers who have lost their land and have the ability to work, with thoughtful considerations, Asia-Potash has offered them jobs in mining companies, vegetable greenhouses and multi-season cultivation demonstration bases according to different situations, and tried its best to create job opportunities for villagers. In the abovementioned village, for example, 21 people were arranged to work in mining factories, 15 in vegetable greenhouses and 26 in multi-season crop cultivation demonstration bases, with 62 villagers resettled, or 64% of the total households.

Fifth, it is dedicated to public service projects for rural revitalization. In terms of public infrastructure, Asia-Potash has helped the construction and development of local villages and built a China-Laos Asia-Potash Bridge of Friendship, improving the travel conditions of local residents. In education, the company funded the building of China-Laos Asia-Potash Hope Primary School for the progress of education. For healthcare, it has provided basic healthcare for poverty-stricken households with diseases, popularized medical and health knowledge among villagers, and set up a healthcare service station with medical kits. In social and cultural terms, Asia-Potash has organized cultural activity centers for the Lao ethnic minority, Makong, in poverty-stricken villages and built more reading rooms with various types of books for primary and middle school students, eliminating the inaccessibility for children in poverty-stricken villages.

III. Achievements and Prospects

First, the income of local residents is increased. Asia-Potash has significantly raised the income of local farmers through the development of multi-season crop cultivation. Compared with the income of only RMB4,600 per hectare of one-season crops, farmer' guaranteed income has tripled to more than RMB13,800 per hectare after Asia-Potash introduced multi-season crops. Moreover, the company has paid great attention to localization and created job opportunities for local people through multiple channels. Local villagers can work in factories during slack periods while enjoying the benefits brought by advanced agriculture. Asia-Potash has contributed an employment of approximately 12,000 people in total, including about 8,000 local employees in Laos, and effectively fueled local economic and income growth.

Guo Baichun, Chairman of Asia-Potash, shakes hands with Lao pupils of the aided primary school

Second, the agricultural competitiveness of Laos is improved. Based on the agricultural mechanization and standardization of the planting process, Asia-Potash has developed a new model of full mechanization and modernization for rice cultivation which is suitable for Laos. At the same time, China's rice quality standards and cultivating techniques are promoted to all provinces, helping Laos to form multi-season rice industrial chains through breeding, planting, processing and export, and driving the transition of rice production from traditional agriculture to modern agriculture. In terms of production equipment, Asia-Potash has introduced the sowing, fertilization and pest control technologies using drones made in China for crop protection to Laos to improve its traditional model towards efficient, economical and sustainable rice cultivation.

Third, local infrastructure conditions are improved. The completion and opening of China-Laos Asia-Potash Bridge of Friendship has effectively reduced the travel difficulties in poverty-stricken and surrounding villages for many years and improved local traffic conditions. The completion of China-Laos Asia-Potash Hope Primary School has enabled children in the village and nearby villages to go to school. The healthcare service station has made medical treatment accessible to local villagers.

Fourth, it has created an "Asia-Potash model of poverty alleviation" that can be replicated and promoted. Asia-Potash's poverty alleviation projects by developing industries, which highlight the leading role of science and technology and the integrated development, have truly changed the traditional model of thinking and ideas of agriculture in Laos and satisfied the villagers' aspiration for a better life. The annual vegetable output of vegetable greenhouses built locally can generate an income of about 1.2 billion Lao Kip. The national leaders of Laos and heads of Khammouane Province have visited poverty-stricken villages multiple times and given high praise and evaluation. Asia-Potash has been established as a good example of poverty alleviation by developing industries by the government of Thakhek district.

Going forward, Asia-Potash will continue to focus on the rural development and poverty reduction of Laos, step up investments, and share China's experience and model of poverty reduction with Lao people, contributing to the agricultural and rural development along with the Government of Lao PDR.

6

Financial Resources Empower Enterprises to Go Global

—Financial Institutions Support Enterprises in Their International Cooperation

Financial Resources Empower Enterprises to Go Global

—Financial Institutions Support Enterprises in Their International Cooperation

In response to the "Belt and Road" Initiative, more and more enterprises have been "going global" in recent years. However, it is difficult for them to expand their business in the international market by relying solely on their own strength due to the numerous capital demands and risk challenges encountered during their international cooperation. In line with the requirements of financial support for the international development of the agricultural industry, financial institutions represented by Agricultural Bank of China and China Construction Bank have made great efforts to form new working ideas and develop financial products, playing an active role in promoting international cooperation of foreign-related agricultural enterprises.

I. Basic Information

Chinese enterprises are generally confronted with the challenges of narrow financing channels, difficulties in financing and high cost of financing in the implementation of the "going global" strategy. Because they are newly established, overseas Chinese enterprises can hardly meet the financing conditions of foreign banks in terms of credit and guarantee. As a result, their liquidity and investment capital needs can only be met by the follow-up financing of domestic enterprises. Currently, indirect financing mainly based on loans from financial institutions remains the main channel for enterprises to raise capital, but there are some problems such as serious shortage of direct and indirect financial support and lack of export credit loans. Meanwhile, the capital needs of overseas enterprises are mainly met by means of offshore financing against domestic guarantee, while the approval procedures for this way of financing are cumbersome and the financing cost is high. The above financing needs are found in the international development of Guangdong Guangken Rubber Group Co., Ltd. (hereinafter referred to as "Guangken Rubber") and China Hainan Rubber Industry Group Co., Ltd. (hereinafter referred to as "Hainan Rubber"). The financial institutions represented by Agricultural Bank of China and China Construction Bank have been taking actions in meeting the financial demands of related enterprises, offering sufficient support for their overseas cooperation.

Guangken Rubber, a natural rubber planting, processing and sales enterprise founded in 2002, boasts an annual output of two million high-quality rubber seedlings, a natural rubber planting area of 650,000 *mu* in China and an annual output of more than 200,000 tons of natural rubber. As one of the three natural rubber production bases in China, the Group has fine qualifications and excellent development prospects. In recent years, Guangken Rubber has been actively implementing the overseas development strategy to expand its production scale. It has established large rubber processing plants, production bases and trading companies in

Thailand, Malaysia, Indonesia and Singapore, currently owning 17 overseas subsidiaries. With the continuous expansion of the Group's production and operation scale, the status and role of overseas subsidiaries of the enterprise are becoming more and more important. Maintaining stable production and operation and sufficient liquidity of overseas subsidiaries has become one of the important tasks of the Group.

Panorama of Guangken Rubber's overseas plant

Guangken Rubber has, with an eye on Singapore's economic and geographical advantages, set up a subsidiary in Singapore, responsible for daily production and sales, overseas financing and expansion of production scale. The Singapore subsidiary in the period of expansion needed a large amount of capital investment in construction. As most of the upstream and downstream clients of the Group were well-known enterprises, and their payment settlement cycle was fixed, the speed of capital flow could not keep up with the capital expenditure needed for expansion. In addition, the purchase demand of a new batch of natural rubber in the overseas subsidiary was close to the payment deadline, and it was necessary to meet the foreign payment on time. As most of the funds collected earlier had been used for the enterprise to expand production, and the domestic group could not allocate support in time, the Singapore subsidiary was in short of capital temporarily. As the Singapore subsidiary of Guangken Rubber was a new enterprise, it would take a long time and there would be many uncertainties if it applied for credit in an overseas bank. Therefore, it was impossible to obtain financing directly from overseas in a short time. The enterprise facing the risk of compensation for breach of contract was in urgent need of financial support from financial institutions.

China Construction Bank holds a meeting with Hainan Rubber Group

China Hainan Rubber Industry Group Co., Ltd. also finds itself in need of cross-border financial funds and service support in the process of "going global". As the largest natural rubber producer in China, Hainan Rubber, seizing the opportunities offered by the "Belt and Road" Initiative in recent years, has been strengthening cooperation with major rubber producing countries to build long-term strategic relations, having established rubber production bases in Indonesia, Cameroon and other places, and expanding the production scale of the enterprise through mergers and acquisitions. To expand the construction of rubber production bases in countries and regions along the "Belt and Road" and promote the international trade of rubber, Hainan Rubber planned to acquire about 36% of the issued common shares of Halcyon Agri Corporation Limited (hereinafter referred to as "HAC Company" or the target company) in Singapore in 2022. This acquisition was of great significance, as it could effectively expand the industrial territory and improve the impact of the enterprise in the industry and internationally. However, in the process of acquisition, Hainan Rubber was in urgent need of bank financing services such as offshore financing against domestic guarantee, letters of credit, international business refinancing, cross-border financing risk participation, and cross-border direct loans.

II. Main Practices

Financial institutions represented by Agricultural Bank of China and China Construction Bank, in the process of providing financial support for overseas investment cooperation of agricultural enterprises, fully consider the actual demands of enterprises, offer suitable financial products and financing schemes for the enterprises, optimize the internal audit management process, speed up the financing process, and effectively solve "urgent, challenging and immediate" problems encountered by the enterprises going global to expand their reproduction abroad, thus supporting their development.

Develop a safe and fast financing plan based on the actual situation. In the case of Guangken Rubber, Agricultural Bank of China introduced the solution of offshore financing against domestic guarantee to the customer by analyzing its transaction background and considering the layout of overseas branches of Agricultural Bank of China. A domestic branch of Agricultural Bank of China issued a financing guarantee with Guangken Rubber as the applicant and the Singapore branch of Agricultural Bank of China as the beneficiary of the guarantee, and the Singapore branch of Agricultural Bank of China provided short-term loans. In the case of Hainan Rubber, China Construction Bank fully considered the characteristics of cross-border M&A, such as the presence of many uncertainties and urgent capital demand, and specially handled Hainan Rubber's overseas M&A financing as a key matter, so that the enterprise would not miss the M&A opportunity.

Optimize the process to improve the efficiency of financing approval. In the case of Guangken Rubber, due to the strict internal requirements for account opening management and the urgency of financing, it was proposed that the loan should be repaid as soon as the enterprise had sufficient funds. After learning about the above needs, Agricultural Bank of China carefully reviewed the process and sought the assistance of the bank at the upper level. The Guangdong branch and sub-branches worked together at multiple levels, to closely cooperate with the Singapore branch, saving the time for the enterprise to open an account. It took less than 20 days for the project to develop from initialization to implementation. In this way, the financial institution provided timely financial support for the enterprise's production and operation, alleviated its short-term financial pressure and helped it avoid the risk of compensation for breach of contract. In Hainan Rubber's case, according to the financing needs of the enterprise, China Construction Bank cooperated with the Head Office and branches, set up a special working team with quick response. After the solution was finalized, the credit application materials were quickly written. Thanks to internal-external connection, the *Due Diligence and Risk Assessment Report on Cross-border M&A Loans* was completed within a few days, which passed the evaluation by the evaluation team and was submitted it to the Approval Department of the Head Office.

III. Achievements and Prospects

First, help enterprises develop and constantly enhance their international competitiveness. With the financial support of Agricultural Bank of China, the overseas enterprise of Guangken Rubber tided over difficulties, obtained stable and sufficient fund flow and successfully expanded its market shares. In recent years, Guangken Rubber, free from worries about the shortage of funds, devoted itself to improving its product quality, optimizing its product structure and enhancing the international popularity of the brand. More than 80% of its products have been supplied to the top 100 tire enterprises in the world, and the application proportion of its products in aerospace and other national defense fields is constantly increasing, occupying the main high-end domestic markets in China. With the support of China Construction Bank, Hainan Rubber acquired about 1.086 billion shares of HAC Company through agreement transfer and mandatory offer (accounting for 68.1% of HAC's issued common shares). After the acquisition of HAC Company, Hainan Rubber quickly acquired the overseas processing capacity of natural rubber and latex, further enhanced the enterprise's voice and influence in the international natural rubber market, acquired the downstream customer resources of the target company, and further integrated into the global natural rubber trading system by using the European and American trade network of the target company. Against the backdrop of financial support, the rubber enterprise "going global" has gradually developed overseas. While promoting the development of local industries, the enterprise has integrated their development achievements into local economic and social development, actively offered international public welfare services, played an active role in solving local employment and supporting the children of agricultural workers to go to school, setting up a good image of the enterprise in international cooperation and enhanced its international influence.

Second, diversify the experience-based models of financial support for agriculture-related foreign cooperation. In the process of supporting Guangken Rubber, Agricultural Bank of China obtained a comprehensive understanding of the foreign-related business situation, development trend and capital demands of the enterprises through various channels to strengthen its professional service. The bank has by far established a three-level linkage professional marketing team of provincial branch and sub-branches to provide its clients with differentiated services such as policy consultation and exchange rate analysis, constantly improving its service awareness and service level based on client needs. Through Hainan Rubber's M&A business, China Construction Bank (CCB) has gained an understanding about the needs of foreign-related enterprises, become familiar with the process and requirements of loan financing for foreign-related enterprises, established a method to analyze and judge the prospects of loan financing projects for foreign-related enterprises, and developed financial products for loan financing for foreign-related enterprises. CCB supports agriculture-related enterprises to go global and become bigger and stronger in the international market through such products as international business refinancing and cross-border finance links. Through cross-border tax refund loans, credit guarantee loans, and export loans, the bank provides small and micro high-quality agriculture-related export enterprises with online pure credit-based cross-border fast loans to solve the problem of difficulties and high cost of financing for such enterprises. Meanwhile, the bank also strengthens cooperation with agriculture-related enterprises in the whole industrial chain, and provides the CCB "Global Matchmaking" financial service platform for free trade pilot zones, comprehensive bonded zones and cross-border economic cooperation pilot zones.

Third, improve the commitment of financial services to the overall situation of agricultural diplomacy. Agricultural Bank of China takes advantage of developed global system resources to realize "one point access, global response", fully leverages the advantages of comprehensive finance and services related to agriculture, rural areas and farmers, and makes good use of the wholly-owned industrial service systems with "on-balance-sheet + off-balance-sheet", "domestic + overseas", "commercial bank + investment bank" and "offline + online" modes to broaden the financing channels of multinational group enterprises, increase international financial supply, fully support enterprises to go global without worries, serve real economy precisely and effectively, and meet enterprises' high-quality development demands with better cross-border financial services, making financial contribution to implement the "Belt and Road" Initiative. China Construction Bank has endeavored to build three capacities, that is, "further enhancing the capacity for serving the country, the capacity for preventing financial risks and the capacity for participating in international competition", giving full play to the advantages of integrated operation and integrated service to link internal and external resources and link the Head Office with branches, diversify the financing tools of M&A loans, financial leasing and corporate credit debt (including short-term financing notes, medium-term notes, asset-backed notes, and rural revitalization notes, etc.) for agriculture-related enterprises, and constantly reduce costs and increase efficiency, in efforts to introduce a new dynamic for improving the comprehensive competitiveness of enterprises and high-quality development of industries.

In the future, relevant financial institutions will further implement the specific requirements of "optimizing import and export trade and foreign investment financial services, strengthening international cooperation, and supporting powerful and prepared agricultural enterprises to 'go global'", strengthen product innovation and optimize the approval process in efforts to provide financial guarantee for the international development of agricultural enterprises in China.

7

Exploring a New Model of "Food Security" Supply Chain

—Aiju Sino-Kazakhstan Grain and Oil Cooperation Project

Exploring a New Model of "Food Security" Supply Chain

—Aiju Sino-Kazakhstan Grain and Oil Cooperation Project

Food security is among a country's most fundamental interests. In 2016, Aiju Grain and Oil Group, in response to the "Belt and Road" Initiative, went abroad to establish the Agricultural Products Logistics and Processing Park in North Kazakhstan Province, exploring a new mode of "Belt and Road" food security supply chain by building a domestic and international high-quality grain "dual-circulation" broad channel, and setting up a model for friendly exchanges between China and Kazakhstan.

I. Basic Information

Xi'an Aiju Grain and Oil Industry Group Co., Ltd., formerly known as Xi'an Huafeng Flour Mill founded in 1934, is a time-honored grain and oil enterprise, and is currently a national key leading enterprise in agricultural industrialization and a national supply chain innovation and application demonstration enterprise. "High-quality grain source region" has always been a focus of Aiju Group. The nutrient-rich black soil in Kazakhstan is 1.5 meters deep with excellent natural conditions, but the grain yield per *mu* is 150-200 *jin*, far lower than that in the United States and China. Kazakhstan, boasting one of the pure lands for green and organic agricultural products, has a very promising development prospect. In 2015, Aiju Group actively responded to the "Belt and Road" Initiative, and finally determined to set a new grain source base in Kazakhstan after repeated research and considerations of various factors. In December 2015, witnessed by the leaders of China and Kazakhstan, Aiju Group and the government of Kazakhstan signed the "Agreement on Investment Cooperation with Kazakhstan". In May 2016, Aiju Group began to build the Agricultural Products Logistics and Processing Park in North Kazakhstan Province. Covering an area of 5,000 *mu*, and with a planned investment of RMB 2 billion yuan, the park is divided into five sectors, including the sector of grain and oil production, storage and food processing, the sector of cattle and sheep breeding and beef and mutton processing, the sector of rural tourism, the sector of industrial technical service, and the Chinese commodity exhibition hall. By far, an investment of about RMB 200 million yuan has been made to build an oil factory with an annual processing capacity of 300,000 tons, two grain depots with a total storage capacity of 150,000 tons, four special railway lines with an annual logistics capacity of 500,000 tons, 1.5 million *mu* of contracted farming of wheat, rapeseeds and sunflower seeds, two drying towers with a daily processing capacity of 1,000 tons and two oil extraction workshops with a daily processing capacity of 500 tons. The Agricultural Products Logistics and Processing Park of Aiju Group in North Kazakhstan is by far the only agricultural processing food project in the "List of Capacity Investment and Cooperation between China and Kazakhstan", receiving close attention and vigorous support from governments at all levels in Kazakhstan. The park has by far received RMB 32 million yuan of local subsidies and RMB 80 million yuan of low-interest loans from local banks.

II. Main Practices

Actively promoting the "Belt and Road" Initiative, Aiju Group attempts to build a "double circulation" broad channel for domestic and international high-quality grains, having built a "closed-loop" supply chain system covering the whole industry with "North Kazakhstan Province, Alashankou and Xi'an" as three bases, opened up the logistics supply chain between China and countries along the "Belt and Road", especially Central Asian countries, and developed, through exploration, a new model of food security supply chain services along the "Belt and Road".

First, pioneer a new path and create a new image of "Aiju" in China and Kazakhstan. Overcoming severe winter cold, Aiju Group managed to build the largest oil factory in Kazakhstan, the first phase of the Aiju Agricultural Products Logistics and Processing Park in Kazakhstan, in only half a year with an annual processing capacity of 300,000 tons of oils, performing a miracle in Kazakhstan's infrastructure construction and establishing a good image of Chinese enterprises. In half a year, the enterprise realized the first full-load return trip of "China-Europe Freight Train". About 2,000 tons of non-GMO high-quality oils and fats have been imported from Kazakhstan, expanding the influence of the enterprise and drawing the attention from society and the governments of China and Kazakhstan.

Second, develop new ideas and build a "three-in-one" transnational large logistics and large processing whole industry supply chain system. So far, Aiju Group has built a "three-in-one" high-quality grain logistics and processing system with Aiju Agricultural Products Logistics and Processing Park in North Kazakhstan as an overseas logistics and processing base, Aiju Agricultural Products Logistics and Processing Park in Alashankou, Xinjiang as a "domestic customs clearance" transit distribution center, and Aiju Agricultural Products Logistics and Processing Park in Xi'an International Port Area as a distribution center, aiming at creating an effective overseas granary in Europe and Asia, so that grains can be "purchased and transported home". Among them, the Agricultural Products Logistics and Processing Park of Aiju Group in North Kazakhstan Province is an "overseas frontier producing region hub", mainly functioning as "raw material production and primary processing". The park can radiate to North Kazakhstan Province and even other provinces hundreds of kilometers around it domestically, and can connect with the production areas of high-quality agricultural products in West Siberia Plain internationally, importing high-quality wheat, rapeseeds and other raw materials from neighboring countries such as Russia and Ukraine. The Agricultural Products Logistics and Processing Park of Aiju Group in Alashankou Comprehensive Bonded Zone functions as a "domestic transit hub", with a main focus on "intensive processing and distribution transit", having the special function of "domestic customs clearance" and serving as a key node connecting China and foreign countries. Internationally, the park can be directly connected to the Agricultural Products Logistics and Processing Park of Aiju Group in North Kazakhstan, and domestically, it can be directly connected to major cities in China, as well as the Agricultural Products Logistics and Processing Park of Xi'an International Port Area of Aiju Group. Xi'an Agricultural Products Logistics and Processing Park of Aiju Group is a "domestic distribution hub", mainly focusing on "distribution and radiation". Located in Xi'an International Port Area, the only inland port in China, the park is a bridgehead of the "Belt and Road" Initiative, and a leader of the northwest hub, radiating to the northwest and addressing the whole country.

Aiju Group's Agricultural Products Logistics and Processing Park in Kazakhstan

Third, develop new mechanisms and set up new contract agricultural cooperatives. When first renting land for grain planting in Kazakhstan, Aiju Group was hammered by Western public opinions, leading to resistance of the local farmers and unsuccessful attempts. In view of this situation, and taking into account the serious problem of "difficulty to grow and sell grain" in Kazakhstan, Aiju Group began to implement a new cooperative model of contract agriculture featuring the participation of "government + bank + enterprise + farmer + university" and set up a new cooperative of contract agriculture. With the participation of Northwest A&F University, Kazakhstan National University and local farmers, the Group has adopted the mode of "contract agriculture and order-based purchase" to implement a one-stop operation strategy of seed research and development, planting, management, harvesting, purchase, and storage, and guided local farmers as to "what and how much they should plant", thus solving the local difficulty in "selling grains". By way of "advance payment", the problem of grain growing cost of local farmers has also been addressed. Aiju Group's new order-based agricultural cooperation model has created an industrial closed loop, that is, Aiju Group prepays the order payment to a bank, the bank lends loans to farmers, the government offers bank loans a discount, and the government gives farmers planting subsidies and gives enterprises export subsidies. This model has realized a win-win situation for several parties, and has thus been unanimously welcomed by Kazakhstani society. It has gradually established a transnational supply chain of agricultural products connecting China and a foreign country and agriculture and commerce, ensuring a long-term and stable supply of high-quality grain sources for China, and further enhancing Kazakhstani people's goodwill towards China.

Fourth, develop new models and achieve win-win development. Aiju Group is committed to building the Aiju Park in Kazakhstan into an overseas investment platform in China, attracting more Chinese enterprises to set up factories in the park, and then forming industrial clusters. Yangling Agricultural Free Trade Zone is planning to cooperate with Aiju Group to build an overseas park and build the Aiju Park in Kazakhstan into an agricultural park of the state level. In the plan, the park will consist of five sectors: grain and oil production and storage and food processing, cattle and sheep breeding and beef and mutton processing, industrial technical services, Central Asian folk culture and rural tourism, and smart park service center. Over a dozen Chinese enterprises have communicated with Aiju Group and expressed their intention to settle in the Aiju Park in Kazakhstan.

Fifth, develop new management modes and change "going global" to

"**blending in**". Aiju Group attaches great importance to local management. The main employees of the Kazakhstan Park are local people, and the management methods are optimized according to local customs and habits, mainly including moderately increasing workers' wages; increasing various rewards, such as attendance rewards; timely payment of regular wages and payment of overtime wages on the same day; organizing various party activities to strengthen the goodwill of local employees to Chinese people; inviting local key employees to visit and study in Xi'an, China; actively participating in social welfare undertakings in North Kazakhstan Province, such as making donations to build five villas for migrant farmers and build roads for villages, and donating schoolbags and appliances for schools, among others. In this way, the Group blends in Kazakhstan society as a builder, promoting the economic development of the country along the "Belt and Road", and improving people's living standards.

III. Achievements and Prospects

After nearly eight years of exploration and development, the construction of the Agricultural Products Logistics and Processing park in Kazakhstan of Aiju Group has achieved remarkable results, with constant improvement of the output value of the overseas park and gradual upgrading of the agricultural industrial chain. Aiju Group has by far established a high-quality grain order planting base of 1.5 million *mu* in Kazakhstan. Since 2015, over 300,000 tons of non-GMO high-quality oil, high-quality flour and organic wheat have been imported into China, which has greatly improved the quality of Aiju grain and oil. By building a "three-in-one" transnational supply chain, Aiju Group has increased the supply of high-quality grain and food. In recent years, the average annual grain and oil sales of Aiju Group have increased by 5%, and the average income increased by RMB 20 million yuan. According to a preliminary evaluation, the brand value of Aiju amounts to more than RMB 200 million yuan. Aiju products have been welcomed and affirmed by leaders at national, provincial and municipal levels. The "contract agriculture" model has offered a new way for Kazakhstan's "win-win agriculture", well received by all local parties. On August 17, 2018, Nazarbayev, the first president of Kazakhstan, visited the park on a special plane, fully affirming the project as "a model of capacity investment and cooperation between China and Kazakhstan". In 2023, "Aiju Grain and Oil 'Belt and Road' Agricultural Products Supply Chain Service Model" was selected one of the first typical cases of new consumption development in China.

Kazakhstan is not only an important country in Central Asia, but also the first stop of China's "Belt and Road" Initiative westwards. Over many years of hard exploration, Aiju Group has scored remarkable achievements in Kazakhstan, which also made Aiju Grain and Oil an outstanding brand in China's agricultural products market. In the future, Aiju Group will continue to increase investment, strengthen cooperation with farmers in Kazakhstan, and further promote agricultural capacity cooperation between China and Kazakhstan to achieve win-win development.

8

Building the China-Kazakhstan System for Preventing and Mitigating Natural Disasters

—A Bilateral Project for Monitoring and Early Warning Agricultural Drought and Pests

Building the China–Kazakhstan System for Preventing and Mitigating Natural Disasters

—A Bilateral Project for Monitoring and Early Warning Agricultural Drought and Pests

Kazakhstan needs to improve its agricultural management in response to serious disasters and unstable output of grain crops. Therefore, researchers from both China and Kazakhstan work together so that, based on China's technological advantages and experience in big data mining and application services, the side of Kazakhstan can collect and collate historical data of agriculture in its country, and the side of China, while building its integrated spatial-aerial-ground monitoring network for agriculture, independently develops a systematic platform for monitoring and early warning agricultural disasters based on data analysis and model R&D. The cooperation is of great significance for improving detection of disasters on the local grain crops and fostering the application of China's advanced technology in countries along the Belt and Road.

I. Basic Information

With an area of 300 million *mu* (20 million hectares) of arable land,

Kazakhstan is the world's largest exporter of wheat flour and the sixth largest of grains. Ranking third in China's grain import, Kazakhstan serves as China's reserve for grain and livestock products in Central Asia. In December 2019, the president of Kazakhstan visited the China-Kazakhstan Agricultural Big Data Analysis Center built by the CAS Research Center for Ecology and Environment of Central Asia. He proposed that the technology of remote sensing big data should be introduced and applied throughout Kazakhstan. The Chinese Embassy in Kazakhstan paid special attention to his proposal and regarded it as an important task for the scientific and technological cooperation of the two countries. To meet the need of Kazakhstan for cooperation in response to agricultural disasters and in technology of earth observation, the Chinese team carried out studies on the earth monitoring and early warning of drought and plant diseases and insect pests with Saken Seifullin Kazakh Agrotechnical University and the Research Institute of Soil and Agricultural Chemistry, the Academy of Agricultural Sciences of Kazakhstan. Three demonstration zones for wheat monitoring have been established, and the domestic agricultural meteorological stations and ground stations for pest monitoring have been set up. The Chinese team extracted field data of three northern oblasts in Kazakhstan based on its domestically made high-resolution image data and deep learning models, and proposed methods for estimating wheat yield based on drought monitoring. Meanwhile, the team independently developed a systematic platform for agricultural disaster monitoring, which integrated ground monitoring, pest identification, agricultural information extraction, and early warning of drought and blight. It also developed an APP for wild land use and blight survey. These have provided a supporting and exemplary software and hardware platform for preventing and controlling natural agricultural disasters in Kazakhstan.

The project not only helps Kazakhstan improve its capacity in monitoring disasters on grain crops through R&D and demonstration of the monitoring and early warning system, but also advances China's IT service and application in agriculture of Central Asian countries in terms of remote sensing satellites, Beidou positioning system, big data and cloud computing. In 2023, the China-Kazakhstan teams convened the Belt and Road International Workshop on Sustainable Development and Natural Disaster Monitoring, and offered the International Training Class on Remote Sensing Intelligent Monitoring and Management of Agricultural Disasters in Countries along the Belt and Road, which won unanimous praise from the trainees, and trained more than 20 technicians for Kazakh partners.

II. Main Practices

Based on their own national academies of sciences, China and Kazakhstan make full use of respective advantages to carry out R&D and implement agricultural projects. China is superior in remote sensing agricultural monitoring, intelligent agricultural IT application, and equipment R&D, while Kazakhstan is advantageous in traditional ground monitoring, drones and field studies. The two countries have finally cooperated in the integrated spatial-aerial-ground monitoring for large-scale studies on monitoring and early warning of agricultural drought and blight.

Adhering to the principle of mutual respect and seeking common ground while shelving differences, both parties grind in and adjust work patterns, and make full use of the convenient network technologies for implementation of the project. In particular, since the winter of 2019 when the COVID-19 pandemic affected actual personnel exchanges, China and Kazakhstan have built a paradigm of cooperation in research and innovation. The specific cooperation mechanisms are as follows:

First, an institute-level organizational and coordinating mechanism. For the sake of promoting international cooperation, the organizations that implement the project have established an exchange mechanism at the level of the deans of both sides. A specific leadership for the project has been established, on the Chinese side, by the CAS Shenzhen Institute of Advanced Technology and the Research Center for Ecology and Environment of the Central Asia, and on the Kazakh side, by the director of the Institute of Soil Sciences of its National Academy of Sciences, and other university presidents, which holistically manages and coordinates the implementation of the project and personnel exchanges.

Second, a mechanism for data sharing. A spatial-aerial-ground data sharing mechanism has been built on the ground of the China-Kazakhstan Agricultural Big Data Center. The local data collected on ground are preferentially retained inside the country and shared with the Chinese side through the cloud platform of the big data center, while the raw remote sensing data are retained in China and provided overseas through on-site deployment of disaster monitoring system models.

Third, a mechanism for effective communication and personnel exchange visit. On the ground of the institute-level organizational and coordinating mechanism, a mechanism for regular personnel exchanges and visits has been established to improve scientific and technological capabilities and facilitate on-site deployment of personnel from the two sides. During the period in response to the COVID-19 pandemic, effective communication and project progress were ensured through on-line communication and training. After the pandemic, Kazakh personnels have been to China for training while Chinese personnels have paid return visits for research and exchange in experimental zones.

Fourth, a clear responsibility system. Regulated for national data security, the two sides focus on their respective tasks and cooperate with each other. Within the long-term cooperation and exchange framework, they have clarified their tasks, connected ground monitoring equipment and collected some disaster data in history. For example, during their investigation on the experimental field in Kazakhstan, the Chinese team collected more than 300 sample sites for crops such as spring wheat, spring corn, peas, flax, potato, and oil sunflower along the way, providing a large number of basic data for ground monitoring. Following the locust control and research team of the Center of Plant Protection and Biological Quarantine of the Academy of Agricultural Sciences of Kazakhstan, the Chinese team investigated the outbreak of plague of locusts, and determined a locust source covering about one hectare in Almaty. Cooperation was proposed in the following aspects based on actual situations: data collection of ground protection against locusts and other objects; remote sensing and satellite data recognition and drafting; on-site sensor application and testing; software development; drone-related projects and sensor R&D; education, internships and practice; impact of drought and salination on agricultural output; snow depth drafting; and assimilation of crop models and remote sensing data; among others.

III. Achievements and Prospects

First, the information of arable land in the three northern oblasts

and the south part of Syr Darya basin in Kazakhstan has been collected. The total vector area of the Syr Darya is approximately 63,410 square kilometers, including about 34,556 square kilometers of actual arable land with 67 megabytes of vectograph files, and 339,655 pieces of plot. The three northern oblasts of Kazakhstan are Kostanay, North Kazakhstan and Akmola, where a total of 20,925 square kilometers of arable land has been collected with 9.9 megabytes of vectograph files, and 59,210 pieces of plots.

Second, a large number of meteorological data have been collected for Kazakhstan. The three ground monitoring stations built within this project cover an area of 20,000 hectares. One station is located in the national grain production base in Qitai County, Xinjiang, China, including one agricultural meteorological station, which monitors rainfall, air temperature and humidity, atmospheric pressure, total radiation, soil moisture, among others, and one pest monitoring lamp, all of which are working normally. Two other stations are situated in Kazakhstan, including two agricultural meteorological stations and two pest monitoring lamps. At present, the Kazakh partners have received more than 10,000 meteorological data and more than a thousand photos of pests.

Third, assistance has been offered in building a system for monitoring agricultural drought that covers the whole area of Kazakhstan. China has developed for the Kazakhstani partner a system for receiving data from pest monitoring and agricultural meteorological stations. The system has been deployed locally and running normally in on-line monitoring and debugging, meteorological drought monitoring, pest identification and statistics, among others. One remote sensing-based system for agricultural drought monitoring has been developed for the Kazakhstani partner, which has been deployed locally. Using a variety of meteorological and soil drought indicators such as vegetation-temperature and crop health index, the crop drought monitoring and forecasting that cover the entire area of Kazakhstan are made every eight days through remote sensing observations of long-time sequence.

Fourth, an agricultural and socio-economic database of Central Asia has been built. The team collected agricultural and socio-economic data from Central Asia and developed a variety of APPs processing files with the function of automatic translation. With more than 10,000 original folders, more than 100,000 files, and nearly 400,000 pieces of text record, a retrievable agricultural and socio-economic database for Central Asia has been built, accessible to researchers throughout the network. It is China's first database of its kind, which also provides a professional data aggregation instrument.

Fifth, the influence of the project has been expanded by means of conferences and personnel training. China and Kazakhstan worked together to convene the Belt and Road International Workshop on Sustainable Development and Natural Disaster Monitoring, and offered the International Training Class on Remote Sensing Intelligent Monitoring and Management of Agricultural Disasters in Countries along the Belt and Road. To monitor agricultural drought and estimate wheat yield, the Chinese research team trained more than 30 Kazakh technicians in technologies to process remote sensing images and monitor drought. The training has received widespread attention from media at home and abroad, and exerted good international influence.

In view of the cooperation and development in the later stage of the project, long-term and sustained investment is required for agricultural monitoring in Central Asia and building platforms for data mining, management, and release. It is just a point of departure to demonstrate the application of the agricultural big data system. Strengthening the monitoring of agricultural conditions and grain crop disasters in Central Asia, improving the spatiotemporal accuracy of monitoring products, and continuing to collect and collate agricultural and socio-economic data for later data mining are of great significance for the security and stability of Central Asia and countries in this area. On the ground of the Kazakh demonstration, the research team will promote digital agricultural products and applications to all other countries in Central Asia and along the Belt and Road, and at the same time, drive the development of monitoring equipment in Chinese enterprises and enhance China's technological appeal in Central Asia.

A seminar between the Chinese team and the Kazakh researchers

9

Technologically Build a Human Community with a Shared Future

—Foreign Aid through JUNCAO Technology

Technologically Build a Human Community with a Shared Future

— Foreign Aid through JUNCAO Technology

The JUNCAO technology is China's original technology with full intellectual property rights, covering areas such as edible fungi cultivation with herbs instead of wood, ecological governance, JUNCAO and fungus feed, development of biomass energy and material, among others. After being listed in China's foreign-aid projects since 1994, the JUNCAO technology has been introduced to 106 countries. For a long time, Chinese foreign-aid experts, relying on the JUNCAO technology, have served the overall diplomatic interests of the country, actively followed the Belt and Road Initiative, and made positive contributions to building a human community with a shared future.

I. Basic Information

Many countries along the Belt and Road share difficulties in development — scarce natural resources, weak economy, frequent natural disasters, and serious soil erosion and degradation. The JUNCAO technology, typical of effective poverty alleviation, can make comprehensive and efficient use of the three major agricultural resources of light, heat and water, realize the cyclic production of plants, animals and fungi, and help ensure security in ecology, food and energy. With a small investment, it can integrate economic, social and environmental benefits in a short period of time, and suit the development of areas scarce in natural resources and weak in economy. Therefore, China rated the JUNCAO technology as a key technology for its foreign aid in the 20th century. Through decades of efforts, especially driven by the Belt and Road Initiative, the cooperation based on the JUNCAO technology has become a vivid practice for China and all other countries to work together to tackle environmental degradation and poverty, and increase the well-being of people around the world.

II. Main Practices

For an effective demonstration and promotion in recipient countries, China's foreign-aid JUNCAO expert group, based on the needs and productive technology of recipient countries, and targeting at independent development through their emerging JUNCAO industry, has fully demonstrated the JUNCAO industrial chain that combines water and soil conservation, soil improvement, feed processing, and edible fungus production and processing, presenting a new approach of increasing job opportunities and alleviating poverty. For a better demonstration and promotion, the expert group has combined with the promotion system of the local agricultural departments and formed its own featuring four-aspect integrations and five-point measures. The team has also created a "base—flagship site—farmer household" model for promotion. The details are as follows:

First, the four-aspect integrations and five-point measures. The promotion must be integrated with natural conditions, government, people and needs of the local area. The measures taken for promotion include localizing technology, simplifying operation, standardizing production, systematizing industry, and organizing farmer households. Take the Kingdom of Lesotho for example, when deciding to use the JUNCAO technology in cultivation of oyster mushroom, the expert group took the dry climate in Lesotho into full consideration and adopted a semi-bagged soil-sealed model. Technical and operating specifications were visualized, digitized, and simplified so that the local workers and farmers could understand easily and learn quickly. Meanwhile, various on-line communities with regards to JUNCAO cultivation and production, oyster mushroom cultivation, and production of bags for oyster mushroom cultivation were available for the foreign-aid expert group to provide real-time guidance online, and for local farmers to learn from each other. In this way, the Chinese-aided JUNCAO technology could be introduced into villages and households more quickly. With enhanced capabilities in their own development, more local people would be lifted out of poverty, the development of local emerging industries would be driven forward, and a healthy development of ecological environment would be ensured.

Second, the base—flagship site—farmer household model for promotion. A base—flagship site—farmer household model for promotion has been created in Fiji, South Africa, Rwanda, Papua New Guinea, among others. The expert group divided the training into three levels according to different trainees.

Trainees at the first level were technicians with certain basic knowledge who were responsible for local dissemination of agricultural technologies, including agricultural researchers, officials from the agricultural department, and head technicians from various regions. They were expected to quickly acquire and disseminate the knowledge. Apart from the on-site training at the bases and the regional agricultural stations or demonstration sites, the expert group built countryside schools at the flagship sites, where they provided hands-on instructions on everything from selecting cultivation sites and building mushroom sheds to creating the best environment for growth of oyster mushroom by keeping warm, cooling, preserving moisture, preventing wind, and controlling light. The trainees, after acquisition of the knowledge, could guide farmer households in their regions in JUNCAO production.

Trainees at the second level were leading and key agricultural technicians in local areas, including key technicians at demonstration sites and communities, responsible people of cooperatives, key demonstration households, and students from agricultural colleges and universities. Trainees were firstly guided in cultivation and production, during which problems were identified and settled. Centralized regional training in theory would follow so that trainees could have a good grasp of the standardized techniques for high-yield cultivation of oyster mushrooms, and independently solve problems in production.

The third level was targeted at new farmer households who planned to adopt the JUNCAO technology in production. An experiential style of learning was adopted at this level. The responsible people of the agricultural department, cooperatives, associations and other organizations called together trainees to attend centralized regional training in turns. The expert group would firstly arouse interests of the trainees in the JUNCAO technology through visiting the bases and tasting oyster mushrooms. After theoretical lectures, they would experience production in practice to have an initial understanding of the JUNCAO technology, laying a good foundation for their subsequent involvement in the JUNCAO industry.

A Chinese foreign-aid expert teaching JUNCAO technology in the Central African Republic

III. Achievements and Prospects

First, the project has promoted poverty reduction and fostered sustainable agricultural development in recipient countries. China's foreign cooperation through the JUNCAO technology has remarkably served the Belt and Road Initiative, and helped greatly in lifting local people out of poverty, especially in improving the status of local women and increasing job opportunities for young people. This has vividly represented how China assists in international poverty reduction. According to incomplete statistics, the JUNCAO technology has rapidly changed the model of mushroom production in Africa. The cost in production has been cut down by 90%, while the output has more than tripled. The products have been exported to neighboring countries such as the Democratic Republic of the Congo, Uganda, and Burundi. More than 20,000 families (farmer households), having directly benefited from the JUNCAO assistance project, have improved their livelihood. China's foreign-aid expert group through JUNCAO technology and the South African government have provided more than 200 fixed jobs for the unemployed in rural areas through building research and training bases, cooperative flagship sites for mushroom farmers, and demonstration sites for JUNCAO cultivation, which have benefited more than 10,000 households. Having grown from scratch, the local mushrooms, thanks to the introduction of the JUNCAO technology, have become the regular food of the local people, and enriched their nutrition sources. The JUNCAO technology has made an important contribution to local poverty eradication, and been hailed as the model of China-South Africa cooperation.

A Chinese foreign-aid expert teaching JUNCAO technology in Lesotho — local farmers had a good harvest

Second, the methods taught through the project have enhanced the development of scientific and technological industry in recipient countries. China's foreign cooperation through the JUNCAO technology has provided the recipient countries with a substantial amount of training for farmer households, the scientific and educational practice bases and JUNCAO classes for local schools, and long-term scientific lectures on the science of JUNCAO in local universities. In Rwanda, China's experts have offered 57 training sessions on JUNCAO technology, trained 2,064 local people, and demonstrated and spread JUNCAO production to more than 3,500 farmer households. In Papua New Guinea, the JUNCAO technology has spread to 17 regions in nine provinces, with a total of 1,984 people having received training, more than 12,770 farmer households having mastered the technology, and more than 40,000 people having benefited. The Eastern Highlands has made JUNCAO cultivation a pillar industry for its provincial economic development and sustainable development.

Third, the project has been embraced by the people and won high recognition from recipient countries. The JUNCAO technology has blazed a trail for agricultural development based on the Belt and Road Initiative, which has been highly praised by the governments and people of recipient countries. In recognition of their contributions to agricultural development in the Central African Republic, President Touadera awarded six Chinese JUNCAO experts with the National Medal of Gratitude at the 61st National Day celebration held in the capital city Bangui. In Fiji, the JUNCAO assistance project has fully leveraged the superiority of JUNCAO in cyclic utilization. A variety of benefits brought by JUNCAO cultivation have been well received by all sectors in Fiji: it provides sufficient raw materials for mushroom cultivation, effectively alleviates deficiencies of green fodder on local pastures in the dry season, advances the development of husbandry, and sets a role model in governing the local soil erosion. The Ministry of Agriculture of Fiji has taken "optimizing the use of JUNCAO to improve the productive forces of husbandry" as one of the five measures to ensure agricultural development of the country. On March 29, 2019, the JUNCAO technology was included in the *Nadi Declaration* issued at the China-Pacific Island Countries Agricultural Ministers Meeting.

Fourth, the project has promoted cooperation and assisted in China's overall diplomacy. In 1994, the JUNCAO technology was listed as a project for the South-South Cooperation, and a "Prioritized Project for Cooperation between China and Other Developing Countries" of the United Nations Development Program. In 1999, the successful implementation of the JUNCAO technology project played a positive role in Papua New Guinea's diplomatic struggle for adhering to the one-China principle, and helped make Fujian Province, China twinned with Eastern Highlands, Papua New Guinea. Xi Jinping, the then governor of Fujian Province signed the sister province agreement and awarded the first-class merit to Lin Zhanxi, research fellow and inventor of the JUNCAO technology. At present, the JUNCAO technology has, by means of training, education, cooperation and assistance, spread to 106 countries, including many countries along the Belt and Road. At the 73rd United Nations General Assembly held on April 18, 2019, the Permanent Mission of China to the United Nations and the United Nations Department of Economic and Social Affairs jointly convened a high-level meeting on the theme of "The JUNCAO Technology: The Substantive Contribution of the Belt and Road Initiative to Implementation of the 2030 Agenda for Sustainable Development of the United Nations." At the meeting, Chairman Espinosa of the General Assembly said, the JUNCAO technology "has set an example for the development of green economy, and created green job opportunities for local youth and women. It is an important practice to promote agricultural cooperation among countries along the Belt and Road."

Next, focusing on the foreign-aid project of JUNCAO technology which promotes the sustainable agricultural development of countries along the Belt and Road, we will continue to strengthen the scientific and technological studies, and improve the foreign-aid effect of JUNCAO technology. We will enhance our capacity in international dissemination of JUNCAO technology, publicize its important role in agricultural development, poverty alleviation, ecological conservation, green development and other aspects, and tell the "JUNCAO story" well, thus contributing to strengthening China's friendly cooperation with countries along the Belt and Road.

10

Gathering Strengths to Build Chinese Brand for Foreign Technology Assistance

—Technology assistance to Burundi by senior Chinese agricultural experts

Gathering Strengths to Build Chinese Brand for Foreign Technology Assistance

—Technology assistance to Burundi by senior Chinese agricultural experts

Burundi, located in east-central Africa, is a typical agricultural country. Its farming population makes up nearly 90% of its national total. Due to poor infrastructure and backward agricultural technologies among other factors, agricultural productivity in Burundi is low. Agricultural industry cannot supply sufficient farm products for the people, causing severe food crisis in the country. To fulfill commitments by state leaders made at the Beijing Summit of the Forum on China-Africa Cooperation (FOCAC), the Center of International Cooperation Services of China's Ministry of Agriculture and Rural Affairs has carried out the agricultural assistance program to Burundi since 2009 in succession, sending senior Chinese agricultural experts to the country in five phases. The program has greatly facilitated rapid development of rice growing and husbandry sectors in Burundi, and made great contributions to prompting in-depth cooperation between China and Burundi in agricultural sectors and building a closer China-Burundi community of a shared future.

I. Basic Information

The project of technology assistance by senior Chinese agricultural experts is a program under the FOCAC framework. In November 2006, the FOCAC Beijing Summit adopted the *FOCAC Beijing Declaration* and the *FOCAC Beijing Action Plan (2007-2009)*. China promised to send 100 senior agricultural experts to Africa, build 10 demonstration centers for agricultural technologies with characteristics in the continent, and strengthen cooperation with Africa in practical agricultural technology and the development of agricultural human resources. Fulfilling the promises, the Chinese government sent 48 experts in five groups to Burundi in August 2009, May 2012, November 2015, March 2018 and March 2020. The Center of International Cooperation Services of China's Ministry of Agriculture and Rural Affairs has been responsible for the management and implementation. They went to Burundi to provide their expertise in rice growing, agricultural product processing, aquatic products, fruit trees planting, livestock and poultry raising and soil and fertilizer management.

Yang Huade, a Chinese agricultural expert in Burundi, shares his joy of rice harvest with local people.

II. Main Practices

Burundi, a less developed economy, still applied backward agricultural technologies and had poor capabilities in promoting agricultural technologies. Following the guidelines of the FOCAC Beijing Summit, senior Chinese agricultural experts surmounted difficulties, customized working methods based on local conditions, and gave play to their expertise and dedication, exploring and developing new approaches to and methods for foreign assistance in agriculture to less developed countries.

First, the expert team innovatively launched a production inputs fund for growing hybrid rice. Located in the east of the African continent, Burundi has a tropical climate and abundant rainfall. Its natural conditions are ideal for rice growing. Due to low yield per unit area by local rice variety, Burundi has been beset by food shortage. Chinese experts went to survey local fields across 15 rice-planting provinces in the country, and picked eight rice varieties that are suitable for local conditions. This solved a historic problem facing Burundi – rice yield reduction or even crop failure in mountainous areas as a result of rice blast. Localized production of some rice varieties has also been realized. In terms of assistance model, the expert team launched a production input fund for sustainable hybrid rice growing. The fund provides funding for seeds, fertilizers and pesticides needed in growing hybrid rice for the first time, as well as technical instructions and know-how training to farmers. After the rice is harvested, farmers can sell them and contribute the production costs of seeds, fertilizers and pesticides provided by the fund to demonstration village cooperative. The cooperative deposits the money into a designated capital account for production inputs in the next growing season. In this way, sustainable rice growing is realized in the demonstration village. An assistance project is able to boost the growth of an industry, and enrich local residents. People's livelihoods are also improved.

Second, the expert team fostered local youth to grow into leaders in developing local industries for prosperity and experts in agriculture. Burundi lacks talent in agriculture. Those working in agricultural sectors lack know-hows and systematic expertise. Prioritizing training for officials in the Ministry of Environment, Agriculture and Livestock, technicians and farmers, the Chinese expert team has been spreading state-of-the-art ideas on agricultural development and empowering local farmers so that they can take the initiative in development. The expert team gave technical training to demonstration farmers on a regular basis, and encouraged villagers to share the know-hows and pursue common prosperity. The Chinese experts made elaborate plans and launched a mechanism for increasing farmers' outputs and income in a sustainable manner. They chose young farmers who are better educated and willing to serve for fellow villagers and gave them whole-process hands-on instruction so that they can lead fellow villagers in getting prosperous. After continuous instructions for two to three production seasons, the young farmers will have the knowledge for an agro-technician in rice growing. Evrard Ndayikeje used to be an unemployed university graduate. In 2016, the young man joined in the demonstration program for growing hybrid rice launched by Chinese agricultural experts, and became the first agro-technician fostered by the expert team in Burundi. After three years, the young man has grown into the youngest senior government official and a leader in national economic development in Burundi.

Third, the expert team worked to spread agricultural technologies and improve the efficacy and level of foreign assistance. The expert team synergized their efforts with China-assisted agricultural demonstration center in Burundi to multiply the effect of demonstration. Since the demonstration center was put into operation in September 2020, the Chinese expert team has been working closely with Burundi's work group to conduct experiments on hybrid rice and spread agricultural technologies. The expert team combined the 12-hectare China-assisted agricultural demonstration center with demonstration sites, and gave full play to their respective advantages to promote agricultural technologies across the country. They built a seed base to cultivate new rice varieties in the demonstration center, demonstration villages in ecological regions across the country, and demonstration training platforms for spreading mature agricultural technologies. The functions in terms of experiment, scientific research, showcasing of achievements and talent cultivation have been fully exhibited. On this basis, the expert team combined seed development in the demonstration center and platform training with the promotion of rice varieties and know-how training in demonstration villages to improve the efficacy and level of foreign assistance. Leading media outlets in Burundi covered Chinese agricultural experts on many occasions. They include Burundi National Radio and Television. The reporting helped more local people to know about Chinese agricultural experts and promoted China's technology in more areas across the African continent.

Fourth, Chinese experts' initiative was effectively spurred. A sound working mechanism was put in place to ensure the smooth implementation of the assistance program. The Chinese expert team made and implemented guidelines for the management of the expert team working on agricultural foreign assistance, ensuring well-regulated and orderly work and life in Burundi. The guidelines also provided institutional guarantee for steady implementation of various work plans. A mechanism for in-team communication was put in place, and information was shared effectively among team members. After years of development and exploration, the Chinese expert team in Burundi established a sound mechanism for in-team communication. They held regular briefings, parties, and one-on-one meetings and participated in public activities, strengthening in-team communication and solving problems in a timely manner. This enhanced the team's solidarity and enabled it to better fulfill the tasks of foreign assistance. Attention was given to foster team culture and enhance the solidarity among team members. The expert team held a series of team building activities. For example, they cooked in turn, and got together on holidays, effectively enhancing team solidarity.

Burundi's President Evariste Ndayishimiye presents a certificate of merit to Yang Huade, a Chinese agricultural expert sent to Burundi.

III. Achievements and Prospects

When implementing the assistance program, the expert team drew on experience China accumulated in fighting poverty came up with the idea of setting a production input fund to promote hybrid rice. They selected Ninga Village Four in Gihanga of Bubanza Province as the first demonstration village for helping Burundi fight poverty through spreading rice growing technology. The experts implemented the demonstration program, provided know-hows training and fostered local young farmers to lead the poverty fight. Thanks to the efforts, 1,072 villagers in 134 households in the village rid of poverty and realized sustainable rice growing. In 2020, the expert team built 22 demonstration villages for poverty reduction, benefiting more than 31,000 farmers. Burundi's President Evariste Ndayishimiye commended Chinese experts' dedication and achievements. He inspected the demonstration villages on four occasions, and presented a medal of merit to Yang Huade, head of the expert team. The president said the country would include China's assistance program in Burundi's national plan for food safety to boost the development of agricultural technology and industry, increase farmers incomes amid efforts to realize the goal that everyone has food to eat and everyone has money to save, and enhance food supply and food safety. On May 10, 2022, Dr. Deo Guide Rurema, Burundi's Minister of Environment, Agriculture and Livestock presented the award of excellent contribution to the Center of International Cooperation Services of China's Ministry of Agriculture and Rural Affairs, commending the center's contribution to promoting China-Burundi agricultural cooperation.

Burundi's government has been paying high attention to agricultural development. It made poverty reduction and food safety important components of the government's development strategy. It worked to develop agriculture, build farmland water conservancy facilities and improve agricultural technologies to change farmers' backward farming technologies and way of production. China's assistance program will provide long-term guidance on agricultural know-hows, spread agricultural technologies and train agricultural talents in a sustainable manner. It will help Burundi further improve technology in grain growing, enhance grain outputs, secure food safety and accelerate the pace of agricultural development.